Prayers of a Teacher's Heart

Praying for your teacher heart!

♡ Hannah Englut

Prayers of a Teacher's Heart

A Guide to Praying over Your Heart,
Your Students, and Your School

Hannah Brooke England

WESTBOW
PRESS®
A DIVISION OF THOMAS NELSON
& ZONDERVAN

Copyright © 2020 Hannah Brooke England.

All rights reserved. No part of this book may be used or reproduced by any means, graphic, electronic, or mechanical, including photocopying, recording, taping or by any information storage retrieval system without the written permission of the author except in the case of brief quotations embodied in critical articles and reviews.

This book is a work of non-fiction. Unless otherwise noted, the author and the publisher make no explicit guarantees as to the accuracy of the information contained in this book and in some cases, names of people and places have been altered to protect their privacy.

WestBow Press books may be ordered through booksellers or by contacting:

WestBow Press
A Division of Thomas Nelson & Zondervan
1663 Liberty Drive
Bloomington, IN 47403
www.westbowpress.com
844-714-3454

Because of the dynamic nature of the Internet, any web addresses or links contained in this book may have changed since publication and may no longer be valid. The views expressed in this work are solely those of the author and do not necessarily reflect the views of the publisher, and the publisher hereby disclaims any responsibility for them.

Any people depicted in stock imagery provided by Getty Images are models, and such images are being used for illustrative purposes only. Certain stock imagery © Getty Images.

Scripture quotations are from The ESV® Bible (The Holy Bible, English Standard Version®), copyright © 2001 by Crossway, a publishing ministry of Good News Publishers. Used by permission. All rights reserved.

ISBN: 978-1-6642-0909-1 (sc)
ISBN: 978-1-6642-0911-4 (hc)
ISBN: 978-1-6642-0910-7 (e)

Library of Congress Control Number: 2020920262

Print information available on the last page.

WestBow Press rev. date: 10/29/2020

DEDICATION

Dedicated to Amanda Rowberry and Maddy Stanitzke, my
two teacher besties, biggest encouragers, and forever friends.
I'm so thankful teaching brought me both of you!

CONTENTS

Dear Teacher xi
Introduction xv

WEEK 1: YOUR WHY 1
Challenge 1: Your Why..3
Your Teaching...5
Your Influence 7
Your Burden 9
Your Vision...11
Your Prayer Life 13

WEEK 2: YOUR STUDENTS' MINDS 15
Challenge 2: Goal Setting..17
Patience..19
Positivity..21
Perseverance...23
Confidence...25
Humility 27

WEEK 3: YOUR STUDENTS' HEARTS 29
Challenge 3: Define Your Class 31
Respect..33
Kindness...35
Generosity 37
Gratitude...39
Leadership 41

WEEK 4: YOUR STUDENTS' SOULS 43
Challenge 4: Define your Students...............................45
Self-Control..49
Responsibility...51

Wisdom 53

Forgiveness 55

Honesty... 57

WEEK 5: RIGHT NOW 59

Challenge 5: Your Student's Needs...................................... 61

Family 65

Friends 67

Food... 69

Shelter... 71

Education.. 73

WEEK 6: FOR THE FUTURE 75

Challenge 6: The Future is Bright 77

Growth.. 79

Health.. 81

Joy... 83

Future 85

Faith 87

WEEK 7: YOUR SCHOOL 89

Challenge 7: Tell Them!.. 91

Teammates 93

Coworkers... 95

Administrators 97

Support Staff 99

Leaders.. 101

WEEK 8: STUDENTS' INFLUENCES 103

Challenge 8: Love in Action.. 105

Cafeteria Workers... 107

Custodians.. 109

Bus Drivers 111

Parents 113

Resource Officers 115

WEEK 9: YOUR HEART 117

Challenge 9: Your Light 119

Your Walk 121

Your Family 123

Your Rest 125

Your Impact 127

Your Love 129

My Prayer For You 131

Reader's Discussion Guide 133

ESV Bible Verse Index 137

About the Author 139

DEAR TEACHER

Like most first year teachers, walking into my classroom for the first time that school year, I had no idea what to expect. I had spent the past few years learning all about effective instructional practices, differentiation, setting up a classroom, and so much more. That summer, I spent my days planning, preparing, decorating, and learning all about what was to come, but nothing truly prepares you for the moment when you have 25 students looking at you, waiting for your direction. Or the moment when you are told, "here are the standards… plan a week of instruction." Or the moment when a parent messages you about grades or discipline or an incident on the playground. Or when administration walks in for your first observation. College doesn't teach you all of that. It doesn't prepare you for all that is to come.

That first year of teaching, I was on a grade level of only four teachers and two of us were fresh out of college. I ended up having both special education and gifted students in my classroom, which is my heart and passion, but it was a little overwhelming at first. I was also placed on several different committees and teams, partly because I was at a small school and everyone wore a variety of hats, but partly because I have a really hard time saying no.

At that time, I had also just started graduate school online and was getting married in just a few months. I guess those are pretty important as well!

That year was overwhelming and exhausting, but also one of the most amazing years of my life. A year of change and growth. A year of getting to know my first group of students and doing all the "first year teacher" things. A year of craziness and chaos. A year I know I will remember forever.

I thought the craziness would settle down after the first year or so, but as I headed into my second and third years of teaching, I found a lot of it was still the same. Talking to veteran teachers, I can't

xi

tell you how many times I've heard, "it never gets less interesting. It never settles down." It seems like each year, no matter how long you've been teaching, we stress about the same things and celebrate the same successes.

Even as I am writing this right now, teachers across the nation are learning a whole new world of education, digital learning. In a matter of days, we have had to transform our classrooms from in person to online with no notice or preparation, but we made it happen because we love our students and love what we do.

All that to say...

I see you. I know you. I am in your shoes. I am pretty sure I can guess and relate to most of the emotions you are feeling right now.

No matter the region, state or county you are in, we face similar challenges and frustrations as teachers. Time. Planning. Assessments. Standards. Technology. Meetings. Data collection. And yes, not even being able to go to the bathroom when the need arises, unless you have a rockstar co-teacher or team teacher to switch off with.

But we also face similar successes and joys as teachers. The everyday smiles that our children bring. Those lightbulb moments. Teaching a child a new skill. When a student learns to read. Watching a child grow and mature. An opportunity to learn something new each day. Truly knowing at the end of the day YOU are making a difference.

It makes it all worth it. Because despite the craziness and chaos that teaching brings, one thing I do know is that every teacher loves his or her students. We all chose teaching, or teaching chose us for a reason. We love what we do, and we love showing up for our kids each day. That's why we are teachers!

I want to help deepen and strengthen your love for your job and for your students. I want to share something to uplift and encourage not only the students in your classroom and the people you work with every day, but your teacher heart as well, because I know it gets weary.

Over the next nine weeks or so (and hopefully years of teaching) you will have the opportunity to read a verse of scripture, a takeaway/application, and a prayer from my teacher heart. Feel free to say, change, or create your own prayers along the way. My situation may not be the same as yours. Your school, class, and students may look different than mine, but each of our journeys is rooted in the same love for our students and love for teaching.

Join me as we surround our hearts, schools, classrooms, and students with prayer over the next few months, remembering that God has placed you in your classroom with each one of your students for a reason, and you are making a difference every single day.

INTRODUCTION

*Show yourself in all respects to be a model of good works,
and in your teaching show integrity, dignity, and sound
speech that cannot be condemned, so that an opponent
may be put to shame, having nothing evil to say about us.*
— TITUS 2:7-8 ESV

Have you ever thought about the impact you have on your students each and every day? We all have an impact on those around us, but as a teacher, that impact is even greater, especially on those 20-30 (or maybe way more) smiling faces we see every single day. Not only are we impacting their learning, but we are impacting their growth and development. We are modeling behaviors and attitudes that these children pick up on and then begin to apply in their own lives. Whether we know it or not, there are always little eyes watching us to learn about not only academics, but about life in general.

Think about your impact. How do you use it? Are you doing more than teaching content to your students? Is there education past the basic subjects and standards? Have you ever truly thought about the impact you make on your student's lives? I bet you can think back and remember some of your teachers and the impact they made on your life. I know I can.

Teaching is a hard job full of lesson plans and testing and observations and conferences and so much more. But God gives us this amazing tool of prayer that we can use to communicate with Him. We can share our heart and listen to what He has for us and for the lives of those around us.

Whether you pray for your students every single day without fail, you've never thought about praying for them, or if you're somewhere in between, like me, this prayer guide will take you through praying for yourself as a teacher, your students, and your school. There will also be little challenges along the way to make you think deeper about

XV

your students and your job, and help you acknowledge areas where you need more support. As you move through the next few weeks you will begin to grow in your capacity to pray and love on your students. That's what teaching is all about, right, learning and growing?

I pray this guide fills you with strength and power as you step into your classroom each day. I hope it overwhelms you with compassion for your students, seeing them in a new light, in God's eyes, as a chosen group of children just for you. I hope this prayer guide makes a difference in the way you teach and the way students learn in your classroom.

I am praying for you on this journey and can't wait to hear how God uses you, your students, and your school over these next few weeks.

CHALLENGE #1

Your Why

> *As each has received a gift, use it to serve one another, as good stewards of God's varied grace*
> — 1 PETER 4:10 ESV

Each of us has received a gift from God, and if you are reading this, then I am sure we share at least one gift in common: teaching. We are called to serve others with our gifts, and in our case, we serve our students and our communities. In order to give the most to the students in your classroom, you first have to dig into the reason you became a teacher, your calling from God. Find your why or your purpose.

How did you know God was calling you to be a teacher? Was it clear or something you struggled with? What made you decide to take this teaching job? Of this particular grade level or subject? What drew you to this area or this school? It didn't happen by accident.

I know in my case, I wanted to be a counselor, but I heard God saying, "Imagine how many kids you can impact each year as a teacher." So, I changed my major to teaching and when I graduated a family friend of mine knew the principal at a school near where I grew up. The principal called me before interviews even began and told me how excited she was to interview me. When I stepped into the school, I knew that was where I was supposed to be.

Three years later, I can see God had a plan then and He still has a plan now! I am not where I am by accident. Neither are you!

Challenge #1- Your Why

What about you? When did God call you to teach? Why are you in the location, school, or grade level that you are in? What drew you there? Being rooted in your why brings purpose and passion in praying for your students.

Today, take a second to jot down your why, and over the next few weeks, keep coming back to it to find strength and encouragement as you pray over your students.

Dear Lord,

I want to first thank You for the gift of teaching. I pray that You will renew in me my calling and desire to teach Your children, Lord. I pray You will keep my heart and mind centered around my purpose for being in this school with these students around me. I know that nothing happened by accident or by chance, but You put me in this place to be an influence on these children. You separated each child out just for me knowing I would be their teacher and their leader for this year. You placed on my heart a desire and a calling to teach, and I am here, following Your calling Lord. I pray on all of my days, but especially on my hard days, You would remind me I am here for a reason, to fulfill Your will for my life and for these 25 kids looking up at me each day. Keep my feet grounded in the foundation of You and Your purpose for my life and the lives of my students.

In Your name, amen

YOUR TEACHING

May my teaching drop as the rain, my speech distill as the dew, like gentle rain upon the tender grass, and like showers upon the herb.
— DEUTERONOMY 32:2 ESV

I wanted to start out the first official prayer for this week, beside the challenge, with this verse that I think I have claimed as my new favorite verse for this season I am in, Deuteronomy 32:2.

I just love how Moses, the writer of Deuteronomy, compares teaching, or doctrine, to rain. Gentle, tender, showers. Not rough, mighty storms.

I imagine our students being the grasses and herbs, waiting for the morning dew and gentle showers to grow and become refreshed. The Lord allows this as a blessing to enhance the beauty and strength of those waiting and willing to receive what He has to offer. Just like with our students, looking to us, craving knowledge and our teaching. We hope our words come like rain, to refresh our students and provide them an opportunity to grow through what they have learned in our classroom.

That doesn't mean that there won't be storms, or rough days, along the way. It doesn't mean that every lesson will be perfectly planned and executed. It doesn't mean that our students won't have to fight to learn and grow every single day, but it does mean we provide them with everything we can to reach their longing for learning, and we will provide it in a gentle, tender manner.

I think about my classroom and the environment that I want to create for my students. I think about my teaching and how I hope it impacts students and their growth. I think about my behavior management and a child's reaction to rewards and consequences. I think about every single thing that goes into making my classroom mine, and this verse comes to mind.

Let my teaching be exactly what these children need. Let me teaching be like rain, Lord, gentle, tender showers.

Dear Lord,

I pray that going into these next few weeks, You will not only renew within me my purpose and desire to teach, but You will also show me what it means to have my teaching fall as rain, gentle and tender. Show me how my teaching is impacting my students and even others in my school building. Help me teach like You, Lord. Give me grace, patience and understanding. Give me strength and a calm spirit. Lord, I pray that You would allow my teaching to reach each one of my students. Not only that, but I pray my actions, behaviors, and words will be an example of that gentle, tender teaching. Use me, Lord, to teach Your children.

In Your name, amen

YOUR INFLUENCE

A disciple is not above his teacher, but everyone when he is fully trained will be like his teacher.
— LUKE 6:40 ESV

You are the biggest influence on your students each and every single day. You have the power to influence their learning, development, character and growth. When you stand up in front of your students or call them to the carpet and begin to teach them about reading, writing and math, you have their attention. All eyes are on you. They want to hear from you. They want to learn from you.

Even walking through the hallway, the kids all around you are listening to you, watching you, and following your example. You have an influence without even trying, without even thinking about it.

Luke 6:40 explains that a student will grow up to be like his teacher. Although our students have many teachers or influences in their lives, wouldn't you want to be a positive one? If you were the only teacher's influence that mattered, how would your students turn out? What would they look like "fully trained"?

One very small example of this is that I greet my students at the door each morning and say "Good morning, happy (day of the week)" in an upbeat voice. Before long, I noticed my students doing the same thing. I even had a student tell me they missed my greeting when we went to digital learning.

Your students are always watching. They notice your behaviors and even mimic them sometimes.

As we go through this prayer guide, think about how you are influencing your students. Do you notice them following some of your behaviors? How can you make sure the influence they are receiving is a good one?

Dear Lord,

I pray that you will help me to fully understand the influence I have on the students in my classroom each and every day. Remind me that I have the power to shape the minds and lives of these students now and for the future. I pray that You will guide me in using that influence for the good of each one of them. Help me to be a role model, an example, of how to live and how to love like You do, Lord. I pray that You will guide my kids to listen and follow the example I set before them. As You guide my heart, behaviors, and actions, I pray that You will guide theirs in the same way. Being a teacher has power, and I want to use that power for You.

In Your name, amen

YOUR BURDEN

Therefore, my beloved brothers, be steadfast, immovable, always abounding in the work of the Lord, knowing that in the Lord your labor is not in vain.
— 1 CORINTHIANS 15:58 ESV

I hesitated to put the word "burden" in this section title because the word is often used in such a negative light, but a burden is the weight we carry, typically a heavy weight. The weight can be a hardship or difficulty we are walking through that we would rather put aside, but it can also be something we choose to carry, regardless of the weight, because we love Christ and love His people.

As teachers, the word "burden" sums up most of what our job is. We carry a heavy burden to teach and to love children each and every day. We carry the burdens that our students, teams, schools and communities carry because we are so deeply rooted in our profession and workplace. We hold them on our shoulders and our minds, hoping to, even just slightly, ease the burden of a child's mind.

This burden is something we live with every single day and, to be honest, one we sometimes wish was a little lighter, but we are in this job for a reason. We choose each day to carry the weight that comes with teaching. It's a burden we know is for the good of so many others.

It's a burden we don't mind carrying, most of the time.

In Galatians 6:2 ESV, Paul writes "bear one another's burdens, and so fulfill the law of Christ." We carry the burdens of our students. We carry the weight that is on their hearts and the unspoken burdens that fill our classrooms.

We are called to do so in order to fulfill the law and love of Christ. Your work has a higher purpose. Stand strong even when the burden feels too heavy. God's got you!

Dear Lord,

It may be unusual to pray, but I want to thank You for the burdens that You have laid upon my heart. I want to thank You for the opportunity to be in a position where I can bear a child's burden, so they don't have to do it alone. I am also thankful for a community in which we bear one another's burdens. As teachers, we go through so much, and it is so nice to know I am not in it alone. There are others who feel exactly what I feel.

I know the world looks at a burden as a negative thing, and I completely understand why. They are heavy, difficult to carry, and wearisome, but it is also such a blessing to be able to go through something heavy or difficult with someone else who understands the load. Lord, I pray, as a school and as a class, we would bear one another's burdens, encourage and lift each other up when we need it most, and be there to sit and grieve when that is needed as well. Use this to unite our school and our classroom. Use this to challenge my heart and make me feel more empathetic towards those around me.

In Your name, amen

YOUR VISION

*Let the wise hear and increase in learning, and
the one who understands obtain guidance.*
— PROVERBS 1:5 ESV

I know you know your students. I know each year, you pride yourself on learning who they are, not only academically, but as a person and a child of God. I know, despite all the craziness of teaching, your students come first, and you want to make sure they feel safe and loved in your classroom. That's why you're here. That's why you are praying over you, your students and your school.

However, praying for your students and truly knowing them goes beyond that, beyond their academic level, beyond their interests and hobbies, beyond their home and family life, into the deepest parts of knowing who they are, what their story is, and what they need. That kind of knowledge can only come from God giving you the vision to see and a mind to understand all that He has to share with you about each one of your students.

Proverbs 1:5 describes a wise person as one who listens, wants to gain knowledge, and obtains guidance from others. Over the next few months of praying for your students, listening to God and understanding His guidance will be key to helping you have the vision to see the things you can't see on your own.

Pray to be able to see God's vision. Pray that He will open your eyes, ears, and minds to see more than what everyone else around you can. Pray that He gives you guidance on what to pray for, how to pray, and maybe even who to pray with.

Dear Lord,

I thank You for what You have allowed me to see, hear and know so far about my students. I thank You for the ability to get to know each one of them, but I want to go deeper, Lord. I want to know how You see them. I want to get to know my students and pray for them because I could be the only one in their life that is talking to You on their behalf at this moment. Allow me to be the person who lifts each one of them up in prayer. Allow me to use these next few months to better understand each student as a child of God rather than just a child in my classroom. Give me the vision to see and guidance to understand what each of my students needs and allow me to be a vessel to serve You and show Your love.

In Your name, amen

YOUR PRAYER LIFE

*Is anyone among you suffering? Let him pray.
Is anyone cheerful? Let him sing praise.*
— JAMES 5:13 ESV

I love this verse because it describes two actionable responses in life: pray and praise, and as Christians, we do both in our daily lives.

As you step into this prayer guide, there are going to be days that you are on fire for God, you are loving every moment with your kids, and you are full of energy when you step in the classroom. There will be days you will feel the power of prayer and want to share with the world. There will be days you will easily be able to praise God for all of the good around you.

But it is not always going to be perfect. There are also going to be days that you are tired, worn out and overwhelmed. There are probably going to be days when you don't feel like teaching, let alone praying for your students. There are days that you want to put on a video and call it a day.

Those are the days that matter. Pray anyways.

In good times and bad times, on good days and bad days, God wants to hear from you. He wants to hear your heart cry out over your students. He wants to listen.

So, commit to praying, every day for the students in your classroom. Pray God will make a difference in your life. Pray He will make a difference in the lives of each student in your classroom. Pray He will make a difference in your school.

Just pray. Everyday.

Dear Lord,

I know there are going to be good days and bad days in the near future. I know there are going to be days where I wake up excited to pray for my students and head into my classroom, but there are also going to be days where I want to stay in bed and ignore the urge to pray or even get up. Lord, prompt me to pray. Lay it on my heart. Give me the strength to wake up each morning and pray for my students. I am committing to pray to You for my kids over these next few weeks. Hear my heart, O Lord, listen to my prayers. Make a difference in my life and the lives of my students. I know You can do anything, and I look forward to seeing what You have in store for us.

In Your name, amen

Week Two
YOUR STUDENTS' MINDS

CHALLENGE #2

Goal Setting

> *May he grant you your heart's desire*
> *and fulfill all your plans!*
> — PSALM 20:4 ESV

Teachers are no strangers to goal setting. From my undergraduate degree into teaching and leadership roles, I know I set goals all the time. I also know as teachers, we set goals with our students. Some of those goals come in the form of learning targets or "I can" statements while others may be more student centered and individualized based on academic content or personal interest.

At my school, we focus heavily on getting students into a goal-setting mindset. Homeroom teachers use goal setting folders with their classes each year and non-homeroom teachers are paired with targeted students to meet, talk through, and encourage them as they set and follow through on their goals. If you walk down the hallways, especially at the beginning of the year, there are student goals all over the walls.

Outside of teaching, everyone sets goals all the time. We set professional goals, academic goals, fitness goals, health goals, relationship goals, etc. Why not set goals for praying over your students?

Challenge #2 - Goal Setting

Over the next few weeks, what do you want to see in your heart? In your students? In your school? How can God move and transform areas in your life? What are small steps you can take to prepare your heart and mind for this journey of praying over your students?

Maybe you want to set a goal of consistency to be in the word and in prayer over your students and school each day. I know that is something I need to focus on in my walk with Christ and on this prayer journey. Maybe you want to focus on an attitude of thankfulness for the many blessings God has given to you like a job, students and the wonderful gift of teaching. Maybe you want to journal each day about your students and about your time with God. Maybe you want to invite others to pray with you. Whatever it is, set your spiritual, personal goal for these few months, and God will do the rest.

Dear Lord,

As I go into this next phase of praying for my students, Lord, I am setting a goal to be consistent in reading Your word each and every day and to be consistent in praying over my students each and every day. I know it is so easy to fall into a place where I want to push off prayer or push off my time with You because the things of the day seem more important, but I want to make a conscious effort to put You first each morning. You are most important, Lord. I want and need to start my day with You, grounded in Your truth. Lord, help me be consistent, not only over the next few months, but always. Keep my heart rooted in You first and everything else will fall into place.

In Your name, amen

PATIENCE

*Rejoice in hope, be patient in tribulation,
be constant in prayer.*
— ROMANS 12:12 ESV

*And let us not grow weary of doing good, for in
due season we will reap, if we do not give up.*
— GALATIANS 6:9 ESV

There are two verses chosen for patience today, one dealing with hard times and the other dealing with reaping benefits of doing good. We all experience times when we must display patience, and as a teacher of little ones, even more so.

We must show patience when teaching a new, unfamiliar concept. Something that may come easy to us, may be new and uncomfortable for our students. For third grade, one of those topics is multiplication. What we can do easily, students are just beginning to learn. This is an example of patience in a hard time. Students are struggling and we are working, modeling and trying everything we can to help them understand.

Other times, we patiently await the outcome of the hard work we have put into teaching our students. From formative assessments to observations to parent conferences and teacher appreciation week, as teachers, we wait and hope for a positive outcome.

Our children have to be patient as well, but it may look a little different. They patiently wait for your directions or your attention or their grades. They patiently wait in the cafeteria for lunch or to use the restroom. They display patience in their own way, and we may not recognize it because those things come natural to us.

Dear Lord,

I've always heard the saying patience is a virtue, and as I grow, I realize how important it is. Lord, I pray that you will help me remember to be patient when I am dealing with a tough situation, but also when I am waiting for the reward of my labor. I pray that you will allow me not to continuously think about what is to come but focus on what is right in front of me. Help me be patient with parents, coworkers and administration.

Most importantly, Lord, I pray You would help me to be patient with my students and let them know that patience is a good thing. Lead me in situations where I can show what patience looks like and open up conversations about what it means to wait in the good seasons and in the bad seasons.

In Your name, amen

POSITIVITY

*A joyful heart is good medicine, but a
crushed spirit dries up the bones.*
— PROVERBS 17:22 ESV

Alongside many of the other character traits we will explore and pray over, positivity is one I hold near to my heart. A joyful heart is good medicine. I think sometimes we just need a positive, joyful attitude to change things and to make any situation better.

I remember in one of the first meetings I went to as a new teacher, we read an article about finding the positive people, or marigolds, as the author called them, in the building and surrounding yourself with those people. I hadn't realized it at the time, but the coworker that called me several times out of the blue during the summer was one of those people for me. She has such a sweet, giving spirit and is always there when I need a friend. Positive is an understatement.

I began to think about how that could translate to my classroom. What if students began to surround themselves with the marigolds of the classroom? The positive kids. The ones that look for the good in every situation. The ones that make them smile and make them feel better. Positivity is contagious. What a difference it could make in our classrooms and communities.

Dear Lord,

Use me to be an example of positivity today and every day for my kids. Remind me to greet them with a smiling face at the door in the morning, kind responses throughout the day, and a positive comment as they head out of my door in the afternoons. Remind me to be encouraging when they need it and even when they don't because I know that positive feedback will go so much farther than correction.

Surround me with positive people, Lord. Show me the good in every situation.

Guide me in having a conversation about choosing positive friendships and being a positive friend to others. Help me choose my words to be uplifting and inspiring. Touch the hearts of my students today. Keep their hearts, minds, and words positive towards themselves and others. Surround each of them with positivity and allow them to find the good in everyone and every situation.

In Your name, amen

PERSEVERANCE

And let us not grow weary of doing good, for in due season we will reap, if we do not give up.
— GALATIANS 6:9 ESV

How many times have you started a lesson to realize it is not going as planned? Your students are looking at you with blank stares. You are stumbling trying to find the right words to explain what you are teaching. And at just that moment, administration walks in for your observation. What do we do? We take a second, gather our thoughts, and switch gears. We don't stop, but we adjust and then keep moving forward, making the best of the situation at hand.

But imagine if every time you had an imperfect lesson you decided to just stop? I would never get anything taught and I probably wouldn't be a teacher right now. No matter what, we persevere through the craziness and keep going.

With our students, we talk about having a growth mindset and the power of yet, teaching them to continue working hard and to not give up even when things are difficult. In their little minds, sometimes they begin to think that if something is hard to do or reach, they should not try, especially when it comes to academics.

One thing we know as adults is that hard work pays off. In school, at work, and in life we have to work for what we want and a lot of times that isn't easy work. Teaching requires hard work. Being a parent requires hard work. Anything and everything. It requires hard work to be successful and grow.

Children need to know that their hard work and perseverance matters. They need to know it is important not to give up and not to grow weary even when things get tough, and we can be an example of what this truly looks like.

Dear Lord,

I know there have been so many examples in my own life of times that I wanted to give up, but instead trusted in You and Your desire for my life. I can't even imagine how different my life would be if I hadn't trusted that my hard work would pay off. Each moment that I continue to decide to not give up, is a moment I know will eventually lead to something bigger and better for my life.

I hope that in my teaching, small groups and talking with my kids, that you would help me bring up the importance of working hard and not giving up on difficult tasks. Help my students realize that just because they may not be successful the first time, doesn't mean they are not strong or smart enough. It just means they are learning. Life takes perseverance. Not everything will be easy, but we have to give our best shot in all that we do.

In Your name, amen

CONFIDENCE

I can do all things through him who strengthens me.
— PHILIPPIANS 4:13 ESV

I admire confident people. Those who set goals, push through and work hard for their dreams. Those who seem fearless and flawless. Those who may have no idea what they are talking about, but can make anything sound wonderful. Confidence is something I struggle with even as I know I am following God's plan.

I think of confidence as being confident in your own abilities. Believing you can do or accomplish something. But technically that is the definition of self-confidence, so the other half of that is confidence in others. Believing that others can and will do what they say they can or will. Trusting in another person.

Both are so important for life. You have to believe in yourself, but you can't do everything alone, so reliance on others is a key part of surviving.

We have confidence in our coworkers to help with planning. We have confidence in administration that they will support us. We have confidence in our coaches and support staff to guide and support our instruction. We have confidence in bus drivers, custodians, cafeteria workers, etc. to do their best to keep our students safe and healthy. We have confidence in our students that they can learn, grow and accomplish so many things while we have them in our classrooms and in the future.

We rely so much on confidence in our everyday lives, but that confidence must come from the Lord who provides our strength.

Dear Lord,

I pray for confidence in myself as I step into the classroom each day. Confidence that I am capable of teaching my students content and making a difference in the lives of the children in front of me. I pray for confidence in my teammates and administration for collaboration and support. I pray they have confidence in my ability to teach my kids and complete my responsibilities on time.

I also want to pray for the confidence of my students. Help them to believe in themselves knowing that they can accomplish so much and achieve anything they set their mind to. Allow them to know that it is okay not to be good at everything, but to find what they enjoy, work hard, and be confident in their abilities. Bless my students with the confidence that can only come from You.

In Your name, amen

HUMILITY

Humble yourselves, therefore, under the mighty hand of God so that at the proper time he may exalt you.
— 1 PETER 5:6 ESV

Hand in hand with confidence, comes humility. Sometimes we view confidence as being proud and seeing ourselves above others, but that's not the case. You can be confident and humble at the same time. Confident in your abilities, confident in others, but not confidence over others.

I love that the Lord can use anyone, but in this verse, He calls us to be humble under his hand, so that he can exalt us or use us for His greater power. So many times throughout the bible God calls those who are not powerful or popular. David. Moses. Noah. Gideon.

God can and will use anyone because He wants to show how great He is within us, not how great we are without Him.

It gives such hope to know that God can use an ordinary teacher, just like you or me. God can use a child. God can use anyone and everyone. He chooses to use the humble. The one that has potential but isn't prideful. The one who is willing to be used by Him, in His timing.

Dear Lord,

I pray that You would help me to see myself as more than just a teacher. Instead, allow me to humble myself before You so that, as a teacher, you can use me as a vessel for Your work here on this Earth. Allow me to understand and recognize my talents and gifts that You have given me and use those gifts to glorify You, Lord.

Along with confidence in their own abilities, I pray my students are filled with humility. There is so much pressure being young, figuring out who they are and trying to prove themselves. Lord, I pray that You would allow my students to see that they are filled with so much purpose and You want to use them in a mighty way. Help them to be humble and lift others up.

In Your name, amen

CHALLENGE #3

Define Your Class

For we are his workmanship, created in Christ Jesus for good works, which God prepared beforehand, that we should walk in them.
— EPHESIANS 2:10 ESV

We are God's workmanship, individually and as a group. We are created by Him, but we are also placed together by Him.

Every year is a little bit different. Some years seem easier than others. Some groups seem more advanced than others. Some are more organized. More talkative. More energetic. More creative. Each group comes with their unique characteristics as individuals and as a class.

God knew which students He was putting in your classroom before rosters were being created, even before these children were born. God had a plan prepared long before we even had an idea that we would be teachers.

He placed these students in your classroom. He placed them together for a reason. Maybe He is trying to make you stronger. Maybe He is showing you patience. Maybe He wants you to lean on Him. Maybe He is giving you a chance to breathe.

We may not know the reason, but God has a purpose for bringing these kids together in your four walls.

In order to dig into this purpose and why God may have placed these students together in your classroom, I want you to define your class. It is completely okay if you feel like this is a hard year. It is completely okay if you feel like this is an easy year. Saying it out loud to God is so much more powerful than holding it in or sharing it with a coworker. God knew what He was doing.

Challenge #3- Define Your Class

What is your class like this year? How would you describe your group of students? Why? Defining your class will help you begin to pray for your students and the needs that you see. Once you share your thoughts with God, you can be open to hearing what He sees and what He has planned.

Dear Lord,

I want to thank You for the kids you have placed in my classroom this year. I know that You placed each one of them here for a reason and You put them all together for a reason as well. You didn't give me this class by accident. You had a plan before I even stepped into this room. As I face challenges with these students, I pray that You would help me see those challenges as an opportunity to learn and grow. Maybe You are trying to teach me patience, kindness, or understanding. Maybe You want me to not sweat the small stuff and focus on just loving them for this year I get to have them with me. Teach me, Lord. Show me what You would have for me as their teacher. I pray that You will use me to be an example of who You are this year.

In Your name, amen

RESPECT

So whatever you wish that others would do to you, do also to them, for this is the Law and the Prophets.
— MATTHEW 7:12 ESV

It's the golden rule, right? Do unto others as you would have them do unto you. I can hear my mom saying it to me when I was little. I can hear myself say it to my students on the playground. "How would you like it if he/she did that to you? It probably wouldn't make you feel good, right? What could you do instead?"

Respect is a popular word when we are teaching or creating rules. Around the world, almost all schools have some sort of motto or saying to help students remember to be respectful towards others, but what does it look like to a student? We can't just say be respectful and all students know exactly what we mean.

As a teacher, we must model and teach respectful behavior to our students. Outside of our four walls, they may not experience respect or know what it looks like.

We teach our students to be respectful of others' feelings by modeling kindness, acceptance, and consideration. We want our students to put themselves in the other person's shoes to think about how they might feel in that situation. We teach them to be respectful of the school's materials and our classroom materials by recognizing their value and purpose.

It is a hard concept to grasp for younger kids, but one that will take them far in life if we teach and model what true respect looks like.

Dear Lord,

Today I want to lift up the children in my classroom. I know that they may be young and not fully understand how their actions affect other people, but I pray that You would help me demonstrate respect for my students. Help me think about how my actions may affect others. Maybe that means not calling on a student who I know doesn't want to speak. Maybe that means listening to a child before jumping to conclusions. Lord, show me how I can show respect to my kids today.

In the same way, Lord, help them to notice my actions of being respectful. Help me to be a model of this behavior. When a situation arises, help me to demonstrate what it means to be respectful and how important it is to notice and think about the feelings of others. I pray that You would help me build up students who are respectful of their peers, adults, and of You, Lord.

In Your name, amen

KINDNESS

*She opens her mouth with wisdom, and the
teaching of kindness is on her tongue.*
— PROVERBS 31:26 ESV

We talk so much as teachers. We speak wisdom to our students, but we also speak and teach kindness. Proverbs 31:26 says "kindness is on her tongue" meaning the words that we speak matter and have the ability to show kindness towards others.

Kindness is a word that is so hard to describe, but you know it when you see it. As an adult and as a teacher, kindness might look like grabbing someone breakfast on your way to work, holding the door open, helping a coworker bring in supplies, sharing an encouraging word, etc.

When I think of kindness in my classroom and with my students, I think of giving compliments, being friendly, picking up a student's belongings that have dropped on the floor, offering to grab something for a partner, and the list goes on.

There are so many little ways to show kindness, but it all comes from a kind spirit within, a kind tongue, and wanting to be a helpful, generous friend.

How can you show examples of kindness towards your students and notice the kindness of others? I believe kindness can truly change the world and it can definitely change your classroom, especially by using our words.

Dear Lord,

I pray that You would help me to be kind today. Use my words not only to teach my students content, but also to teach them kindness through the words I choose, my tone of voice, and body language.

Help me focus my lessons and small groups on kindness in the form of giving wait time, showing encouragement, giving compliments, acknowledging effort, and greeting each student with a smile. Keep my heart away from anger or frustration, but instead on kindness in my classroom.

Help me to also notice and encourage kindness in my students. I pray that You will let my kids see kindness in me and begin showing it towards their classmates. Help me to address unkind behavior with a gentle response, instead of frustration. With my words, actions and behaviors, show my students that they are loved by You and me.

In Your name, amen

GENEROSITY

*In all things I have shown you that by working hard
in this way we must help the weak and remember
the words of the Lord Jesus, how he himself said,
'It is more blessed to give than to receive.'*

— ACTS 20:35 ESV

God gave His son to die on the cross for our sins. The ultimate sacrifice. The ultimate gift of love and generosity. In my life, God has not asked me to sacrifice something as big as He did, but He does ask us to give. It is so much better to give than to receive.

Give of our time in spending time with Him, helping others, serving others, praying, etc. Give of our money through tithes and helping those that are not as fortunate as us. Give of what we have for His glory and to help others around us. It doesn't have to be big, but God says in Acts 20 that it is more blessed to give than receive.

I think sometimes kids are better at this than we are. I have seen many times, children giving their possessions to others, just because, but I also seen times where children have a hard time giving to others when they want something for themselves.

Giving is something we can easily model and explain through giving of our time and attention in the classroom, snacks when a child forgot his or hers, or even just giving compliments and feedback to others.

Dear Lord,

As a teacher, sometimes I feel like I give all the time. I give my time in the afternoons and weekends to plan, prepare, and pray for these kids. I give my Saturdays and summers to help those who are struggling. I give my mornings and afternoons in meetings or clubs and activities. I give my money to supply my classroom, buy books, and make sure my students have what they need. But Lord, I know that my time is not my own. I know that my money and belongings are not my own. They were given to me by You to use for this purpose, so help me to be thankful for times that I get to be generous because You are so generous to me Lord.

Help me to be an example to my students of Your great generosity, generous with my time, money, supplies and attention. Allow me to show them that it is so much better to give than to receive. As circumstances arise where a child has a choice to be selfish or generous, guide my words in helping them make the best decision.

In Your name, amen

GRATITUDE

Rejoice always, pray without ceasing, give thanks in all circumstances; for this is the will of God in Christ Jesus for you.
— 1 THESSALONIANS 5:16-18 ESV

Rejoice. Pray. Give thanks. These three things are the will of God. Giving thanks goes beyond a simple "thank you." Giving thanks requires an attitude of gratefulness in appreciation of what you have or have received.

I love when I sit down to finish lesson plans to find out one of my teammates has already completed them. I love going into our assessment to finish adding questions to find it has already been finished. I love walking into breakfast at work when I have forgotten mine in the microwave at home. I love opening my computer to send an email just to find out it was already taken care of.

I appreciate all of those little things and I hope that my words and actions show my appreciation to those who make my life easier each day.

We long for others to show us gratitude or appreciation when we do something for them just as they long for us to do the same in return.

But I have noticed so often, that gratitude comes from influence. If you receive gratitude and appreciation, you are more likely to show gratitude and appreciation. If you receive gratitude from your administration, you are more likely to show gratitude back. If you receive appreciation or validation when you help out a teammate, you are more likely to help again and be more appreciative for the work they do.

In order for our students to show gratitude, they need to see us being grateful for the little and big things in everyday life.

Dear Lord,

I pray that You would give me a heart of gratitude. Help me to notice the little things and the big things that people do for me, say thank you, and to truly mean it with my words and actions! Lord, I know that I appreciate it when others show gratitude towards the things I do, so help me to pay that forward, being genuine and kind, making a conscious effort to show my appreciation.

I pray that You would use me to be an example of gratitude for my kids. Help me to notice the small things they do, even if it is turning in their work on time, cleaning their space, being kind to a friend, etc. Show me these things so that I can show my gratitude and acknowledge their heart to build a positive classroom community. Fill the hearts of my students with gratitude every day.

In Your name, amen

LEADERSHIP

He laid aside his outer garments, and taking a towel, tied it around his waist. Then he poured water into a basin and began to wash the disciples' feet and to wipe them with the towel that was wrapped around him.
— JOHN 13:4-5 ESV

I never loved the leadership opportunities when I was growing up, and as an adult, I still don't love the idea of being a leader, most likely because of my worldly definition of what a leader is. All around there are good and bad examples of leaders from our own communities, states and nations. Sometimes it is hard to discern a good leader from a bad leader when the lines get muddy.

My mind goes back to Jesus and the example He showed on multiple different occasions throughout His time on earth.

One of the most notable times Jesus showed Himself as a leader was when He served his disciples by washing their feet at the last supper. Jesus stepped away from His position at the head of the table, to get down on the floor and wash the dirty feet of those who were followers of Him saying "If I then, your Lord and Teacher, have washed your feet, you also ought to wash one another's feet" - John 13:14 ESV.

If we learn anything from His example of leadership, it is that we are called to serve others regardless of the position we are in. Leadership is not about being the most liked. Jesus definitely wasn't. Leadership is not a one person job. Jesus had His Father and the disciples. And leadership is not self-seeking. Jesus served others before himself.

As we are the models and examples of leaders for our students, it is our responsibility to show that a leader isn't someone who is above others or wants to make others feel inferior. A leader is someone who has a heart to serve and love others.

Dear Lord,

I pray that in my school and with my students, You would give me the heart and mind of a leader. Not a leader like the worldly example I so often cling to, but one like the example You provided through Your Son. I pray that in my school, I would not be self-seeking, but that I would look to seek You first and others second. Help me to be an example of what a good leader looks like to my students and those around me in my school.

Allow my students to see me as a leader, not of this world, but a leader like You, Lord. Let me show them who a true leader is and help them to grow into the leaders that You have called them to be. I pray You would show the importance of service and its crucial role in being a leader. Guide my words and actions as I am shaping the future generations definition of the word leader.

In Your name, amen

Week Four

YOUR STUDENTS' SOULS

CHALLENGE #4

Define your Students

So we, though many, are one body in Christ,
and individually members one of another.
— ROMANS 12:5 ESV

My first year of teaching, I remember hearing more seasoned teachers talk about their students. I felt like they knew every intricate detail of what made each student unique- their background, family, prior academic levels, interests, needs, learning styles etc. I was just so amazed by all of the knowledge they possessed about their students.

But I also felt a little inadequate. Why didn't I know my students that well? I knew them, but I didn't really know them like I wanted to when I compared myself to others. I was just trying to survive that first year.

Now, only a few years into teaching, I feel like there are moments where I can tell you everything about one of my precious students, but there are also moments where I might look at you and not be able to tell you a single thing.

I've realized it's about building those relationships, learning about their lives, and investing in who they are as a child, not just a student. At the end of the day, yes, test scores matter. Yes, we hope they are able to master all of the standards, but what's most important are those relationships you build with each and every student in your room.

So, we've defined our classes, now let's define our students.

I am a type-it-up, put-it-in-a-chart kind of person or I will forget

PRAYERS OF A TEACHER'S HEART | 45

it. Recently, I decided to compile all the information I know about my students into one place. It has their names, family information, academic levels, interests, books they enjoy, learning styles, and more. This spreadsheet is huge, but one that I will continue to add to as the year goes on and I learn more about each of them.

While this works for me, it may not work for you, and it may not work for me by the beginning of next year. But I love the idea of having everything I want to know about my students in one place that I can easily access. It helps me remember what makes each of them unique and I can be a better teacher to them.

Challenge #4- Define your Students

What works for you? How do you currently keep track of your students and everything you know or want to know about them?

Maybe you want to use a notebook and put each of your student's names at the top so you can easily access it whenever you want to add information. Maybe you have an About Me sheet they fill in at the beginning of the year, so you make a copy and add notes to that. Maybe you jot quick things down as you are working with students and then go back to organize it later.

This is not a one size fits all system, and it is definitely not a one day challenge.

Today begin thinking about how you can dive deeper into getting to know your students and keeping track of what you learn about each of them. Continue to work on this throughout the year as they grow and you learn more. Use this to your advantage. Invest in their personal lives. Build those relationships. At the end of the day, this is what matters.

Dear Lord,

I first just want to thank You for every single student You have placed in my classroom. Over and over again You have shown me that each child was placed into my classroom for a reason and You set aside each one for me to be their teacher. Lord, I have been praying over my heart and actions to be a reflection on You. I pray every single day that You would use me to do Your will, Lord. I have also prayed over my students individually and who they are becoming. Lord, I ask you now more than ever, help me build those relationships with my students. Help me to dig deeper in finding out who they are and who they want to be. Lead me into situations where I am prompted to learn more and to grow in my knowledge of each of my students. Allow me to use what I know of them to be a strong teacher, confidant, friend and mentor because I know every single person could use a little more of that in their lives. Lord, watch over my students. Watch over my classroom. Keep Your hand upon us.

In Your name, amen

SELF-CONTROL

For God gave us a spirit not of fear but of power and love and self-control.
— 2 TIMOTHY 1:7 ESV

Psychology is so interesting to me, especially child psychology and the inner workings of a child's brain as they develop. While there are many theories on development, we know that starting at a very young age children learn about self-control and how to regulate their own emotions and actions. This is one of the things that teachers of young students, and even older students, focus on in their classrooms.

However, even as grown, mature adults, we struggle with self-control.

Two things come to mind when I think of self-control, or lack thereof. First, I love getting breakfast on the way to work. A sweet tea and chicken minis start my day on the right foot. Do I need breakfast every morning? No. I am very capable of grabbing a granola bar or making a smoothie, but it is a temptation I give into most mornings. Secondly, like many teachers, I have a weakness for children's books, especially those dealing with social emotional needs of students. I can spend hours in a bookstore picking out new books, or I can hear a teacher talk about a book she loves and immediately go online to find it.

We all struggle with self control. Our brains are fully developed and able to determine the difference between what we need and what we want, what we should do and what we shouldn't. Imagine your students. Their brains are still trying to figure it out. Imagine how much harder it is for them to say no, or understand why you tell them no.

It's hard for teachers and students, but God gives us a spirit of power, love and self-control. We must lean on Him in times of weakness. We must show our students that it is okay to not be able to perfectly regulate emotions, actions and desires, but we work towards leaning on the Lord to find strength.

Dear Lord,

I know some of my examples seem silly, but self-control is an area that I sometimes struggle in, and if I struggle with it, I am sure the sweet kiddos in my classroom do as well. Lord, use me as a model of self-control. When I am having a rough day, remind me to lean on You. Help me maintain my composure, be calm and practice controlling my words and actions. Use these moments of frustration or interruption to be an example of what self-control looks like. In all areas of my life, help me practice self-control and lean on You when I feel weak.

I also pray that You will guide my students on understanding self-control in their words, behaviors, and actions. Whether that looks like keeping their hands to themselves or there is a much bigger issue at hand, help me to facilitate sticky situations with understanding and compassion. Allow my students to understand the need for self-control in their daily lives.

In Your name, amen

RESPONSIBILITY

So then each of us will give an account of himself to God.
— ROMANS 14:12 ESV

When our time on Earth has come to an end and we stand in front of God, we will give an account of our lives, our words, our actions, and our behaviors. We are responsible for the way we live our lives.

The same is true on Earth. As adults and as children, our actions, words, behaviors, thoughts, etc. have consequences whether they are good or bad, and we must take responsibility for those things.

Hopefully at home our students have some sort of responsibilities. Growing up, my parents did a great job of teaching me responsibility through chores, helping out the family and being diligent in doing my homework. I'm sure most of your parents held you accountable as well and you are teaching your children the same things.

As a teacher, we have responsibilities to show up each day prepared, teach content to our students, attend meetings and professional development, write lesson plans, etc, but we also teach our students how to be responsible. As students, they are responsible for paying attention and completing their work, being kind to others, cleaning up after themselves etc. Having those expectations at school (and home) sets students up to be accountable and successful.

Dear Lord,

I know that in life I am responsible for the way I live and that one day I will stand across from You and give an account of the life I lived. I also know that in my job, my home, and my life here on Earth, I have responsibilities as well. I was raised and taught to follow through on the things I am responsible for and I know that it is my job to pass that onto these children in my classroom.

Use me to show what it means to be responsible and to begin having those conversations with my students. Whether that means being consistent with classroom jobs, showing them how to organize their belongings and notebooks to keep up with assignments, or helping them understand they are responsible for their own learning. Help my students be accountable for the responsibilities they are given and understand that their actions have consequences, good and bad.

In Your name, amen

WISDOM

*The fear of the Lord is the beginning of wisdom,
and the knowledge of the Holy One is insight.*
— PROVERBS 9:10 ESV

True wisdom comes from God. The ability to understand right from wrong and the ability to make a decision based on that understanding. We have rules and laws in place in the Bible, in our country, and in our classrooms for a reason.

We set classroom rules to help students understand what is expected of them. We model and teach which words, behaviors, and actions are good or right and which ones are wrong or not the best choice.

We have the conversation about rules at the beginning of the year and often revisit when things get a little bit out of hand, but how often do we talk about the reason behind the rules. Things like safety, respect for others, order, etc. From young children to adults, we want to know why we have to do certain things, not just follow blindly.

We can build student understanding of wisdom by teaching them why we have rules and why certain things are right or wrong. Including students in the building of rules at the beginning of the year and with changes throughout the year, helps their understanding of the necessity of rules. This begins to instill wisdom in our students.

Dear Lord,

As I become older, I learn more about right and wrong and I learn more from You and those around me; however, I know I have much more to learn. I pray that You would share your wisdom with me. I want to learn from You and I want to learn about You Lord. Show me right from wrong and lead me towards making the best decisions for Your kingdom and Your children. Make me wise.

Lord, I pray that You would help me begin the conversation of the importance of having rules and knowing right from wrong. Lead me in helping Your children begin to learn the difference in what You would have for them compared to what the world may desire or expect of them. Teach them to look at You and those in authority for wisdom and guidance in their everyday walk.

In Your name, amen

FORGIVENESS

*Be kind to one another, tenderhearted, forgiving
one another, as God in Christ forgave you.*
— EPHESIANS 4:32 ESV

One of the greatest gifts we have received is forgiveness. Forgiveness of our sins and a slate wiped clean in Christ. What a beautiful gift, but also what a beautiful example of how much Christ loves us and what that love looks like.

As I am writing each one of these prayers, I can easily see the areas in which I struggle, forgiveness being one of them. It is so easy to say, "it's fine" or "I forgive you," but it is so much harder to truly forgive someone who has wronged or hurt you. It's so hard to forgive someone when they don't know what they have done, and they don't ask for forgiveness. It is so much easier to hold onto grudges.

When we are children, I believe we forgive easily, maybe because our attention spans are shorter or maybe because the wrongdoings are less significant. As we grow old, we realize that forgiveness is important, so we don't hold onto anger or hurt, and we make the most out of our time on earth (at least I hope this is the case).

But somewhere in the middle, we begin holding grudges. We hold onto hurt and pain. We find it hard to let go of the things of the past. We find it harder to forgive, even though we know holding on causes hurt and bitterness. We want to stay in our pain and frustration, ignoring our calling from God to forgive.

But what an amazing release it is when we finally forgive or ask for forgiveness.

As a teacher who has so much influence, we don't want to make mistakes, but our students need to see us make mistakes and then ask for forgiveness. Our students also need to see us forgive others, especially when they do something wrong.

Dear Lord,

I pray that You would show me places in my heart where I need to forgive and let go of some things and areas in which I need to ask for forgiveness. Forgiveness can sometimes be a daily action such as a hurtful word of a coworker or student. There are things that I hold onto that I know You would let go of, forgive, and move on, but there are also things I may not even realize that I have done and need to ask for forgiveness. Lord, I pray that You would reveal those things to me and open my heart for what You would have me do in each situation.

I pray that You would also help my students understand forgiveness. At this age, some of them hold onto things of the past. Some of them have seen and heard things that I am blessed to not have experienced. I don't know every situation of their lives, but I do know that You offer forgiveness for what they may have done and for what others may have done to them. Guide them in asking for forgiveness and being forgiving people.

In Your name, amen

HONESTY

And you will know the truth, and the truth will set you free.
— JOHN 8:32 ESV

Better is a poor person who walks in his integrity than one who is crooked in speech and is a fool.
— PROVERBS 19:1 ESV

This section of praying over your classroom ends with honesty. It is one of the most popular character traits that teachers and parents hope their kids grow up with (from my small poll of friends and family), but as classroom teachers, dishonesty is so hard to address.

Complete honesty time. When I was in 5th grade, I was doing a writing assignment in social studies. I can't even remember the topic, but I do remember the moment. I was sitting at my desk in the second row, writing my paper, and I couldn't remember the name of one of the Native Americans or Explorers or whatever it was, and I knew my book was right inside my desk. It wouldn't hurt to take a small look, right? I just needed a name. I had the rest.

Wrong. One of my classmates told the teacher and I lied about it. Eventually the truth came out. My parents were called. I had to talk to the principal. I was horrified. Luckily, I had an amazing 5th grade teacher who truly cared about me as a person and was forgiving, but I will never forget that moment!

I think that is why dishonesty bothers me so much! Most of all because being dishonest is so much harder as both the one who is telling the lie and the one who is searching for the truth. Somehow the truth comes out eventually. The truth will set you free. Imagine, the stress in a child's mind about being dishonest. It weighed so heavy on my little heart, so I'm sure it weighs on their hearts.

Dear Lord,

As an adult, I know the difference between the truth and a lie. Sometimes, I know I fall short with little white lies that I think don't matter but I know that they matter in Your eyes and You see it all. I pray that You would help me in the areas where I am tempted to bend or stretch the truth to make it sound better. Help me own up to my shortcomings and mistakes. Allow my words to have a foundation in honesty and integrity. Allow me to be an example to these students.

I pray that You would guide my kids as they are beginning to experiment with telling a lie or not the whole truth. I pray that You would nudge their hearts. They may not know who You are or what they are feeling, but I pray they would feel the importance of telling the truth in every situation. Allow my words to be full of wisdom when they need to understand it is okay to make mistakes, but necessary to tell the truth.

In Your name, amen

CHALLENGE #5

Your Student's Needs

Ah, Lord God! It is you who have made the heavens and the earth by your great power and by your outstretched arm! Nothing is too hard for you.
— JEREMIAH 32:17 ESV

I still have a large sticky note with the goal I set going into my first year teaching, my why or purpose. It was to get to know my students, create a safe environment, and let them know I loved and cared for them each and every day. I know this goal still holds true for me and most teachers each year of their teaching career. Even with testing and data collection and lesson planning and everything else that comes with being a teacher, we try our best to hold tight to these things.

There is only so much we can control, but for the 7-8 hours we have these children, we love and care for each of them. When they leave us for the day, we don't always know what they are going home to, and when they leave us for the year, we may or may not see them again. Either way in both situations, we hope for the best. We hope that our students are healthy and happy and have a bright future ahead of them.

Over the last few weeks, we have prayed over our students individually and as a whole. We have also prayed over our own hearts as well as the people in our school buildings that impact student lives each day. I hope you've seen a change in your heart as you have gone into each day with a heart close to God in prayer, and I hope that you've seen a change in your student's hearts as you have prayed over each one of them.

This next section will go beyond the classroom. Beyond the character traits at attitudes of your students and into their lives at home and in the future. We may not know everything each child is dealing with, what their home life looks like, or what their future holds, but we do know that God is in control and He can do far more than we could ever ask. As you pray over your students during this next week or so, ask God to show you areas of need where you may not be able to see.

Trust in Him. He can do far more than you can ask or imagine.

Challenge #5- Your Student's Needs

Right now, take a moment to write down anything you know might be an area of need for a child outside of the school building. Is there a family who is hurting for food? A mom and dad going through a divorce? A child who is sick, physically or mentally? A situation of abuse or homelessness? Maybe you can't put your finger on it, but you know there is a student you need to pray for. Anything you can think of jot that down, and then begin to pray. If you can't think of anything specific right now, that's okay. As you go through this week, pray God lays on your heart specific things for you to pray for and areas in which you can help or be a witness to your students.

Dear Lord,

I want to thank You again for this group of students You have given me. I am so thankful to be a teacher and have the ability to impact students each and every day. Thank You for giving me this calling and gift that I can use to serve You.

I know that my main goal as a teacher is that my students feel safe and loved. I know I can only control that for the time that they are with me and the rest is out of my control, so I choose to pray. I pray that You would open my heart to the areas in which my students struggle outside of school. I am only aware of a small portion of what each one of them goes through on a daily basis. I pray that You would watch over them, protect them, and love them when I can't. I pray they each have a safe home to go to, a family that loves them, food on the table, and a future that is full of hope and happiness.

Lord, I pray that You would show me specific areas to pray for or general guidance on what each of them need. Show me ways in which I can be an example, supporter, and mentor where possible. Keep my heart focused on You and loving my students.

In Your name, amen

FAMILY

Behold, children are a heritage from the Lord, the fruit of the womb a reward. Like arrows in the hand of a warrior are the children of one's youth.

— PSALM 127:3-4 ESV

During the week, our students spend more waking hours with us, August to May, than they do with their own families which allows us to have a huge impact on their lives, but it also makes the time with their parents and families so much more important because there is less of it.

I know when my husband and I get home from work, we have a few hours together, eat dinner, and then it is pretty much time to start getting ready for bed. I cherish those hours, but they can easily get cut short if one of us works late, has an appointment, or needs to run by the store.

The same is true for our students. Many parents work, travel and have errands to run on a daily basis. Some parents work far away from home, so their commute is time consuming. There are always sports, clubs, and after school activities going on, so the time parents have with their children is often cut short. Our students may be from a one parent home or have multiple siblings who need to be cared for which divides the already short time available into smaller and smaller chunks. There are so many different scenarios even beyond our knowledge or control.

Time is so valuable. Time with family is so valuable but can easily be taken away or taken for granted.

All we can do is pray for our students and their families. For time, safety, happiness, and love among each of them.

PRAYERS OF A TEACHER'S HEART | 65

Dear Lord,

I pray the home lives of my students are strong and safe. I pray they have families that love and care for them. I pray parents are invested in the lives of their children, asking how their day was, and helping them with homework. I pray they have food on the table each night and a warm place to lay their heads. No matter what the situation, I pray each one of my students goes home to a safe and loving environment each night. I pray each need they have is met.

Lord, I pray that You would show me if there is a way I can help any of my students in their family lives. I know this could be a sensitive subject and I don't want to overstep my boundaries, but Lord, show me areas in which I can pray for these students and their families. Show me an area of need in which I can fill. Help me be an example of Your love to my students and their families.

In Your name, amen

FRIENDS

A friend loves at all times
— PROVERBS 17:17 ESV

When I think of friendships, sometimes I put more value in the friendships children have with each other rather than the friendships I have with other adults, but recently God has laid on my heart the importance of building community and friendships at all ages. As adults, we value friendships and enjoy time spent with our friends, but too often life seems to get in the way. We prioritize work and errands and chores over spending time with those who are close to us.

Proverbs 18:24 talks about a friend sticking closer than a brother, and Proverbs 17:17 says that a friend will love at all times.

Think about the friendships you have made in your life. The ones that were there just for a season. The ones that have been by your side from the beginning. The ones that seem to be formed perfectly in heaven. How has your perspective on friendship changed as you have gotten older? Do you still have a childlike love with your friends?

We rely on our friendships to pull us through the rough days, celebrate with us on the good days, and love us always.

I hope my students build friendships now that will last a lifetime, but more importantly, I hope they always have a true friend on their side. A friend that loves unconditionally.

Dear Lord,

One of my favorite things about being a teacher is getting to help my students build relationships with others and getting to help them through the good and bad of those relationships. I am in a position to make a lasting impact on the way they interact with others, so help me encourage collaboration and appropriate interactions. Allow me to show how important it is to build community and have people to count on at any age.

I pray that my students find friendships in my classroom. Although everyone may not always agree, I pray they would be able to be respectful and kind to all and find a few students they can develop deeper relationships with. I pray as my students grow older, they will keep some of the connections they have made at a young age, but they will also continue to develop new friendships in each season of life. I also pray they would find a friend in You, Lord. Allow them to never feel alone. Let each child know that he/she is loved.

In Your name, amen

FOOD

And God said, "Behold, I have given you every plant yielding seed that is on the face of all the earth, and every tree with seed in its fruit. You shall have them for food."
— GENESIS 1:29 ESV

When is the last time you have eaten? Me, I am eating as I am writing this. Most of the time there is either food in my hand or I am thinking about my next meal. My husband thinks I am crazy for planning meals days ahead or thinking about what I want to eat for dinner at eight in the morning.

Food is something I know I take for granted. I can't remember a time where there wasn't food on the table, healthy food, comfort food, a variety of different options to choose from, but I know that is not the case for many people.

No one should have to go without food, especially a child.

I have spent many hours volunteering for food banks and raising money to support those who are in need of food, but I know even with my small efforts and the efforts of those around me, there are still so many children who go without food.

I am so thankful when students come to school, they can eat two healthy meals and there is assistance for those who may not be able to afford buying a school lunch. I am also thankful that so many schools have programs in which children in need are sent home with food over the weekends and holidays.

Today, pray for your students and their families. Pray they would have food on the table now and in the future. Not only ask God to meet their basic needs but go above and beyond. We know God can do far more than we can ask or imagine. Ask God to show you where there may be an area of need so that you can be of support.

PRAYERS OF A TEACHER'S HEART | 69

Dear Lord,

I am so thankful students get to come to school each day, if not for anything else, but to get a meal. I work at a school with an amazing cafeteria staff that works hard to make sure students have two warm and healthy meals a day. I pray students who are in need of food and even those who have food at home take advantage of this opportunity, and if they need assistance paying for food, they will reach out for support.

I pray that You would provide food for my students and their families at home. No matter what the circumstance, I pray they are able to eat dinner each night and three meals on the weekend days. I pray they would not wonder where their next meal would come from, but they would have peace in knowing they will be fed. Lord, if there is a family in need, show me how I can help and be a servant to them and to You.

In Your name, amen

SHELTER

For we know that if the tent that is our earthly home is destroyed, we have a building from God, a house not made with hands, eternal in the heavens.
— 2 CORINTHIANS 5:1 ESV

My first year of teaching I had a student enroll on open house day. I found out that she had just been placed in a new foster home, but they weren't sure how long she would be there. A few weeks later, without warning, she had moved away to her third home in three years, her third school in three years. She didn't take her lunchbox home that day and there was no way of getting it back to her.

I will always remember her and that moment. When I think about her situation, I realize just how temporary the things we have are and how quickly they can be taken away.

It doesn't matter how great or how small the things we have here on Earth, there are far greater things waiting for us in Heaven. We know that God has prepared a beautiful shelter for us. Even if we don't have a physical shelter over us here on Earth, God will always be a shelter over us in tough times.

As teachers, we don't always know what the home lives look like for our students. We have an idea of what the community looks like, but we don't know their socioeconomic status, the type of home they live in, or who lives in the home with the child, and is not our place to know all of the details.

But we can pray that our students have a safe, physical home to go to each night. We can pray for God's protection over them physically and spiritually.

Dear Lord,

I may not know what the home lives look like for many of my students. As far as my knowledge, each one of them has a home to go to each night and I am so thankful for that. I am thankful there is a physical building of safety and security for each one of them. Lord, I pray that You would never take that away from them. Allow my students to always feel like there is a shelter, beyond just a building, they can go to and call home.

Lord, I pray my students' homes are filled with air conditioning in the summer and heat in the winter. I pray my students have a bed to sleep on and clothes to wear. I pray they have running water to bathe in and a yard to play in. Lord, I pray You would supply the needs of each of my students and their families. I pray if there is a need in the community, You would allow me to be a help in the areas in which I can and allow me to pray specifically for that family.

In Your name, amen

EDUCATION

*An intelligent heart acquires knowledge, and
the ear of the wise seeks knowledge.*
— PROVERBS 18:15 ESV

From the heart and mindset of a teacher and being part of a teacher community, we value education. We value learning. We encourage and hope every child has limitless educational experiences and their knowledge increases as they grow older.

I know I have been blessed with the opportunity to attend great schools from elementary all the way up to my graduate degrees. I have been blessed with amazing teachers and professors who not only valued education but had my best interest at heart and wanted to watch me learn and grow.

If you are reading this, hopefully your community is one rooted in a love for education and children as well. Hopefully your district has plans in place to help students continue to learn and grow after high school, whether it be college, the workforce, or other opportunities.

As teachers, we hope to encourage our student's love for learning and pray they seek knowledge as their hearts and minds grow. We influence the process of how they view education and what they choose to do for the rest of their lives.

Dear Lord,

I appreciate the opportunity and luxury of having a strong education. I know around the world, there are children and adults who have not gone to school and don't have opportunities to grow in learning about the world around them. I thank You for the ability and desire to learn and a heart and mind that want to seek and acquire knowledge. I know the greatest knowledge comes from You, Lord, and I pray You fill my heart each day.

Lord, I pray my students love to learn. I pray they value education and see the purpose in being knowledgeable and wise. I pray I can make learning a fun experience so they want to continue to attend school and can fulfill the purpose You have set before them. Lord, I pray for each one of my students as they make decisions regarding their future. Allow them to choose knowledge that comes from You. Allow them a desire to continue to learn. Teach them to be wise.

In Your name, amen

CHALLENGE #6

The Future is Bright

For I know the plans I have for you, declares the Lord, plans for welfare and not for evil, to give you a future and a hope.
— JEREMIAH 29:11 ESV

Sitting in my very first interview, there were about twelve teachers, coaches and administrators around me asking questions about my student teaching experiences, my educational philosophy, my teaching aspirations and how I planned to run my classroom if I was hired.

I can't remember what we were talking about exactly and I can't remember what brought it up, but one of the teachers sitting on the other side of the table said, "they are all OUR students" referring to a couple students she had a few years back. I remember thinking at that moment, "yes, but once they leave your classroom, technically they are someone else's student. Right?"

It wasn't long before I realized that my students really weren't just my students, especially being the collaborative teacher. My students are shared with resource teachers and pull out special education teachers and speech therapists and occupational therapists, just to name a few. Even my gifted and general education students are shared with so many other teachers.

There is no student that belongs to just one teacher, which is amazing to think about because each child has several different positive adult role models surrounding them, rooting for them, and watching them grow.

Although we have many students around the building, our focus each year is on the students in our classrooms each day. While we have them now and while we have our attention focused on each one of them, I want to not only pray for their present, but bottle up prayers for their futures.

Challenge #6- The Future is Bright

Think about your first group of students, the students you've had over the years and the students you had last year. If you could go back in time and pray one thing over their future, what would it be? Think about the students you have now. Think about their lives one, two, five, ten years down the road. What do you hope their lives look like? What can you ask God to do in their lives?

God has a plan for each one of us. A plan of hope, welfare and a future. Why not start praying for the future of our students' lives now?

Dear Lord,

Over the past few years, You have opened my eyes to what it means to share my students with the rest of the teachers in my school building. This may be the reason why You allowed me to be the general education collaborative teacher, so I could learn to view the students in my classroom as belonging to many teachers in the building. Each child is our child. Each child is Your child.

Lord, I pray that You would guide my heart on praying for the future of the students in my classroom. While they are with me, it is easy to see my prayers in action and to change my words and actions to be a servant to their needs, but when they leave, it is so much harder to remember to pray and see my prayers in action. Lord, allow me to bottle up prayers for their future, their families, their careers, their health, their friendships and their faith in You, Lord. Walk with these children each step of the way. Lead them in the path You would have for them.

In Your name, amen

GROWTH

*And though your beginning was small,
your latter days will be very great.*
— JOB 8:7 ESV

In third grade, we talk about point of view and how each author, character, and person has his or her own point of view. Well, as I am writing this, I know my point of view may be different from yours. I have elementary aged students who still have a ton of growing to do, and at first, I didn't think I could share much on the topic of growth for teachers of older students.

Then I realized, I view growth more of a physical thing for my students whereas there are so many other components: socially, mentally, academically, emotionally, etc.

Even as adults, we are still growing every single day. We learn and try new things. We meet new people. We become more confident and brave. We grow in our careers. We are always growing and changing, and so are our students of all ages.

Whereas my students have a lot of growing to do, yours may be reaching their fully grown selves. Maybe they need to grow by refining their skills or finding who they are.

How do your students need to grow? We have prayed over their hearts, minds and souls. We have prayed over their families and relationships. You see them and know them better than almost anyone, so which areas do they need to grow?

Dear Lord,

I pray for healthy growth and development for my students. They are so young and have so much more growing to do physically, socially, mentally, emotionally and academically. As of now, I know their brains are still forming; therefore, they are still learning and developing basic life skills. I pray that as they grow, Lord, they grow in You and towards You. I pray they grow in confidence and respect and self-control. I pray they grow in humility and love and wisdom.

Lord, allow me to aid in positive growth for my students, encouraging social, emotional and mental development of each child. Use my classroom environment and activities to promote a positive, safe place to grow and learn. I pray they grow up into the men and women You would have them to be, Lord.

In Your name, amen

HEALTH

Or do you not know that your body is a temple of the Holy Spirit within you, whom you have from God? You are not your own
— 1 CORINTHIANS 6:19 ESV

In times of sickness, it is easy to pray for health, but when we are healthy, we don't typically pray to stay healthy. We may thank God for our health, but we typically just expect that being healthy is normal.

But we also know how fast things can change. We know how easy it is to get sick. We know how easy sickness can spread around a school. We know that in what seems like just a moment, everything can change whether we are prepared or not.

There are things we can't control in this life. We typically can't control if someone is going to get cancer or have a heart attack or break a bone. Things just happen and they are a part of life, but there are also some things we can control.

We can control what we put into our bodies, if we choose to exercise or not, how we treat ourselves and talk to ourselves.

Being healthy is so much more than uncontrollable sickness. It is about making positive choices physically and mentally every day.

Our bodies are a temple. As teachers, we can help educate our students on what it means to take care of our bodies. We hope they learn good healthy habits and we pray they live long healthy lives.

Dear Lord,

I pray that my students are healthy, physically and mentally. I pray that You would protect them from illnesses that could interrupt their childhood. I pray that You would have Your hands upon each one of them and if anything comes their way, they will be able to fight it with You, Lord. In a world with increasing mental illness, I pray that You would guide and protect their minds from the dangers and pain of this world. Not that nothing bad will ever happen, but that whatever life throws their way, they can handle it with You.

I pray that You would give each one of them the strength to make healthy decisions in their lives. I pray that in times of temptation that they would choose to make the right choices, the healthy choices, knowing that their bodies are a temple and are worthy to be treated well. Guide their decision making and help each one of them stay healthy physically and mentally.

In Your name, amen

JOY

*I perceived that there is nothing better for them than
to be joyful and to do good as long as they live.*
— ECCLESIASTES 3:12 ESV

I pray that my student's basic needs are met. I pray that they have a family and a safe home. I pray they have food on the table each meal. I pray they live a life that is healthy, and they make healthy choices, but I also hope and pray for so much more for my students because I know You can provide so much more.

The Bible says there is nothing better than to be joyful and do good. Happiness is fleeting and dependent upon the moment, but joy is deep down. Joy is something that lasts no matter the circumstances of life. Joy comes from God.

I hope my students are joyful. That they genuinely enjoy waking up each day, spending time with their families and going to school.

I don't know each home situation. I don't know what happens when a child leaves my classroom each day. I know that each student has his or her own hardships and that nothing in life is perfect, but I hope deep down inside that my students are filled with joy now and in the future. Joy that can only come from the Lord.

Dear Lord,

I hope and pray that my students are joyful, that they are filled with joy deep down inside. A joy makes them excited to wake up in the morning, excited to spend time with their families, and excited to learn at school with their classmates and me each and every day. Lord, fill them with joy. Even when things seem to be tough, I pray You would fill each child with a joy that comes from knowing You.

Lord, I pray that You would help me do what I can to be an example and an influence to provide a little bit of happiness and joy in the lives of my students. I pray that You would lay on my heart specific students who need to know what joy looks like in their lives and help me to be an encourager and supporter to each of them.

In Your name, amen

FUTURE

*The heart of man plans his way, but
the Lord establishes his steps.*
— PROVERBS 16:9 ESV

I have the privilege of teaching 3rd graders. At this age, they don't know a whole lot about who they are, what they are passionate about or what they want to do with their lives. Even as an adult, there are some days that I don't know what I want to do with my life, but as a teacher of all age groups, we play an integral part in developing what their futures may look like.

We introduce them to a variety of different content, skills and strategies that they may or may not be interested in or use. We teach them communication skills and interpersonal relationships. We teach collaboration and independence. We begin to build foundations for what they will need in the future and what their futures may look like.

At first, I thought it was kind of silly when people would say that I could be teaching the next president, inventor, or world changer, but it is so true. We never know who the students in our classrooms will become. We don't know who might change the world or who may be teaching right beside us in a few years.

No matter the career path, I hope that my students each have a bright future ahead of them. I hope they find something they are interested in and work towards their life goals.

Dear Lord,

I teach such small children and it is sometimes so hard to think about their future beyond elementary school. I have such a limited scope of the millions of possibilities that await each one of my students as they grow up and move on in life. Lord, I pray for these two things. I pray

You would give each one of my students a passion or interest. I pray You would show them a talent or gift you have given them. Secondly, I pray You would give them the drive and ambition to set goals and to work towards those goals.

I may not know what the future has for each one of my students, but I pray it is bright and full of love and happiness. I pray they grow up to have families and jobs. I pray they would come back one day and tell me all about where they are in life and what they decided to do. Lord, I know that I make an impact on their future, but help me look for and enhance their passions. They are so young, but they are not too young to begin finding what they love.

In Your name, amen

FAITH

Now faith is the assurance of things hoped for, the conviction of things not seen.
— HEBREWS 11:1 ESV

I wanted to end this section by praying over the faith of my students and of your students. Some teachers have more freedom to talk about their faith in the classroom while others in public schools are limited by what they can say.

Either way, we can't make a child have faith in God. We can't make them show love towards others as God loves us. It is a personal decision and a personal connection with Christ. We can't do anything but share and show what God has done in our own lives and pray He will do the same in the lives of our students.

In our classrooms, through our actions and words, we can show the love of God to our students, giving them hope of a future and far greater things that lie ahead. We can also pray over each one of them to have a relationship with God and to follow His plan for their lives. By living out each one of these prayers, we are sharing God's word and God's love with our students without even sharing our hearts.

You are impacting their faith every single day.

Dear Lord,

I pray more than anything else I have prayed over the past few weeks that my students have faith in You and act upon that faith. That they would have a desire to love You and want to serve You. That they would have hope and faith in only You rather than the things of this world. Help them to find wisdom and understanding in You, Lord.

This world means nothing if they don't have You in their lives. You provide shelter, security, love, joy and anything else they need in this life. Far greater than that, You have prepared a place for each one of us to be in heaven with You one day. Lord, I pray that I am a witness of You. I am a light leading them towards You and all that You provide. Lord, call them to You, in Your timing.

In Your name, amen

CHALLENGE #7

Tell Them!

Two are better than one, because they have a good reward for their toil. For if they fall, one will lift up his fellow. But woe to him who is alone when he falls and has not another to lift him up! Again, if two lie together, they keep warm, but how can one keep warm alone? And though a man might prevail against one who is alone, two will withstand him—a threefold cord is not quickly broken.
— ECCLESIASTES 4:9-12 ESV

When working with kids, one of the most popular sayings is "it takes a village," and in the school setting that is no different. Teachers put in so much work for the kids and are with them most of the day, but there are so many others in the school building that have an impact on student learning and development.

Your coworkers, administrators, support staff, cafeteria workers, custodians, bus drivers, and local leaders all work hard to make sure your students are safe, fed, and learning.

Because of their impact on students, I want to lift them up in prayer as well. Along with that, I want you to tell them you are praying for them. Let them know why they are important to you and your students.

Ecclesiastes says that two people are better than one and a cord of three strands is not easily broken. By praying for and supporting the people who work in and around our schools, students are more supported, safe and loved. Students know they can go to anyone in the building to help them in any area of need.

Challenge #7- Tell Them!

As you go through these next few days, take a moment to tell your school people that you are praying for them and you are thankful for the work they do to positively impact students. You can write them a card, bring them a treat or just have a conversation, but tell them! Let them know how much you appreciate their work.

Dear Lord,

I am so thankful to work in a building that cares for and supports students from their emotional and physical well-being to their education. I know that each employee that works at my school wants the best for students and works each day towards making that happen. Thank you for providing me with a school and community of people who love what they do and love students.

I pray that over these next few days you would help me to acknowledge and encourage each of these groups of people as they work to support students. Help them to feel appreciated for their hard work and dedication to students each day, because together we are so much stronger.

In Your name, amen

TEAMMATES

Iron sharpens iron, and one man sharpens another.
— PROVERBS 27:17 ESV

Since I began teaching, I've been on a team of three to four people each year, with a few others such as advanced content teachers and resource teachers that I consider my teammates as well. I don't know any different, but I do know that when working on a small team, you get to know each other real quick.

I assume it is the same in any profession, but as teachers we lean on our teammates so much because planning every mini-lesson, small group, and assessment for every subject is a lot for one person. We need each other to be committed and hardworking not only for us to be successful but for our students as well. We need to be able to trust and lean on our teammates. We need to work together no matter what.

Whether you are on a team of three or twelve, each team has its challenges, but just as iron sharpens iron, we sharpen our teammates and they sharpen us. Working together helps us become better teachers and better people.

Because we are so dependent upon our teams and spend so much time planning alongside each other, we need to pray for them. Pray for your relationships as well as your ability to work together and be successful for the good of your students and your own mental health.

Dear Lord,

Thank you for giving me a team. I don't know if it is like this everywhere, but I am blessed with great teammates and the relationships we get to have being such a small team. I am thankful for the encouragement and challenges of working on a grade level team. Lord, I just want to pray over my teammates. I know this is unusual for me. I pray for specific needs, but I don't pray for them in general. Today I want to lift them up to you. I pray that we will be united and strong working together this year. Allow us to help each other grow and be constructive in our feedback and comments. Lord, allow us to keep positive and respectful in all circumstances. I know there will be times we disagree, but those are the moments that push us to be stronger and better at our jobs.

I also pray for the health of each member of my team and of their families. Allow this year to be one of safety and security, free from overwhelming distractions and pain. If something comes up, Lord, help us support each other throughout this year. You have placed me with this team to be a light and an example of you. Help me to use my role as a teammate to glorify You in all that I do.

In Your name, amen

COWORKERS

Whatever you do, work heartily, as for the Lord and not for men, knowing that from the Lord you will receive the inheritance as your reward. You are serving the Lord Christ.
— COLOSSIANS 3:23-24 ESV

Just like being on a small grade level, a small school has its benefits and drawbacks. One of the most amazing things about my school is that I know each of my coworkers by name and at least a little bit about their lives. I love this, but I also know others who have five or six times the number of teachers in their school, so knowing everyone is next to impossible.

No matter the size of the school, I believe there are coworkers that God put in your life to build relationships, friendships, and strong bonds, but there are also those that are meant to challenge you and help you grow. Some people bring out the best in you while others seem to sometimes bring out the worst, but each coworker is there to make you stronger and sharper.

Every employee of a school is working heartily, with a heart of passion and desire to do good for students. We pour our hearts and souls into our students, and we know that the work we are doing is good. We serve the Lord by teaching children, and we know this work will pay off.

So, lift your coworkers up in prayer and let them know you are praying for them! They are probably facing similar day to day challenges as you and could use all the prayers they can get.

Dear Lord,

I am blessed to be at a great school with great coworkers. I know that I see some more than others and some are easier to get along with than others, but you've placed each one of them in my life for a reason, to help me grow stronger and sharper, and I am so thankful for that, Lord. We are all working together for such a beautiful purpose- to teach and love the children that come into our school. We know this is the work You have called us to do and we want to do everything we can to help students be successful.

Lord, I pray that You would have Your hand upon our school and the teachers inside the building. Allow us to build relationships with one another and truly get to know the people we spend our time with. Allow us to be able to count on each other and work together well. I pray that You would keep each of my coworkers safe and healthy. Be with their families and their home lives, Lord. I pray that they can step away from their jobs when the school day is over and spend time with the ones they love.

In Your name, amen

ADMINISTRATORS

It shall not be so among you. But whoever would be great among you must be your servant.
— MATTHEW 20:26 ESV

My first year of teaching, I was hired by an amazing principal. She was such a strong, professional woman, but also had the kindest heart. She saw the potential in people and pushed them towards seeing it in themselves. She was someone I knew I could come talk to when I was overwhelmed or stressed. She always knew the right thing to say at the right time, and she truly wanted the best for students and teachers.

She retired after my first year at the school, and I am not sure if she will know just how much of an impact she had on my life in that short amount of time. Words can't explain who she was and what she meant to me.

Since then, I have been blessed with another amazing principal as well as two wonderful assistant principals.

I don't think many people graduate college thinking they are headed into school leadership and administration. Some do, but I've heard many teachers felt a calling to make an impact on a larger scale as an administrator.

Being completely honest, it is not a job I want, but I so admire those in administrative positions.

I am not sure if it is because we are a small school and everyone knows everyone or if all teachers see this, but administrators work so hard to serve others! I can't count the number of times I have seen my administrators running from one place to another, juggling a million different things. They give of themselves every single day working for us, students, their parents, and the school.

School administrators are truly special people, and they deserve our love and prayers.

Whether you are blessed with amazing administration or you have had a rocky relationship with your administrators, pray for them. Your prayers may look different than mine, but God wants to hear from you, the good and the bad. He wants to hear your heart.

If you are struggling to find peace and common ground, pray about that. If you are looking for a time when they are not distracted to talk about your goals or struggles, pray about that. If you need to bring something to their attention and you are not sure how, pray about that. If you love them and are so blessed, then thank God for that.

Today, pray for your administration, and let them know you are praying for them!

Dear Lord,

I have been so blessed to be at a school with amazing administrators. From my first year of teaching to now, You have placed wonderful role models in my life for me to look up to and come to for anything. Lord, I just thank you for them and for the impact they have had on my life. I know they are not put in an easy position, but they do so well under their everyday pressures to serve others. I know I am so blessed to have each one of them.

I want to lift my administration up to You, Lord. I pray that You would give each of them the strength to push through each day and handle whatever life throws at them. I pray that You would guide their decision making, keeping their hearts and minds on You and our students. Help them to do what is best for our students each and every day. I pray that You would keep the joy and passion alive for educating and supporting educators, because they make such a difference. Allow them to know that they are loved and valued in their positions.

In Your name, amen

SUPPORT STAFF

Therefore encourage one another and build one another up, just as you are doing.
— 1 THESSALONIANS 5:11 ESV

It is probably called something different at different schools and different counties, but I like the term support staff- those people whose main job is to support teachers as they support students, or to support students in an area of need. People like literacy and math coaches, gifted and ESOL teachers, reading recovery, early intervention, resource teachers, etc.

All of these people hold a special role in education, and whether your school has one or fifteen, they are so valuable to teachers and students.

Last year, a new literacy coach transferred to our school about halfway through the year, and she was so positive and encouraging. Everything she did was to build my capacity as a teacher to help me better teach my students.

I can't tell you how many times I met with her and other coaches or support staff around our school to get ideas, plan, and monitor student progress. I am so thankful for the extra work they put in to help teachers and students be successful.

Today, pray for your support staff, whatever that may look like at your school. If you don't have specific people to support you and your team, think about where you go in your school or county to receive support, and pray for them. Don't forget to tell them you are praying for them and let them know how much you appreciate all they do.

Dear Lord,

I am blessed with wonderful support staff at my school, people to encourage and build me up as a person and as a teacher as well as help support and encourage students. I know this is something not all other schools have, but I am thankful for the opportunity to work with others and receive support from them when needed. Thank you for surrounding me with coaches and other teachers. I know in this profession, I am not alone.

Lord, I pray You would bless them and keep these teachers and staff members encouraged in their position. I know their work can sometimes be overwhelming and underappreciated, but they are so valuable for teacher and student success. I pray You would allow them to see the growth of students due to the time and work they put into providing support to others. Keep them safe as they may travel to different schools. Allow them to know just how appreciated they are.

In Your name, amen

LEADERS

Moreover, look for able men from all the people, men who fear God, who are trustworthy and hate a bribe, and place such men over the people as chiefs of thousands, of hundreds, of fifties, and of tens.
— EXODUS 18:21 ESV

I want to end this section praying for our school leaders. Local school leaders and administrators are so important and valued, but so are district, state, and country leaders. These people impact schools on such a large scale. We don't often pay attention to them when things are fine, but as soon as something goes wrong, or we don't agree with a decision they make, everyone knows their names.

I can't imagine having to make educational decisions for a whole county or state. The pressure is unimaginable. How do you decide what is best when it seems like opposing viewpoints are both strong and supported? How do you take the pressure for making a wrong decision? How do you know what is truly the best choice for all people involved- students, teachers, parents, and community members? I'm so thankful I don't have to make those decisions, but even more thankful for those who do.

I love that this verse calls leaders those who are able, those who fear God and those who are trustworthy. Our school leaders need to be these three things, and as Christians directly impacted by their decision making, it is our job to pray for them and over them. It is also our job to respectfully voice our opinions to help them make the most informed decision.

Dear Lord,

I pray for the men and women who are in leadership positions in my county, state, and country. Lord, I can't imagine the pressure they feel to make decisions that benefit students the most while keeping in mind parents, teachers, and the community, especially the decisions that aren't easy and may be taken negatively. I pray that each one of these leaders would fear You, Lord. Allow them to make decisions based on what You would have them to do. Give them wisdom to see the big picture that we as teachers may not see at the moment.

I pray in the decision-making process, our leaders will be honest and trustworthy, making decisions for the best of each student, district and state. Keep their eyes, hearts, and minds on You. Lead them. Let them know they are appreciated by those they serve. Even if we disagree, we are thankful for their leadership and heart of service.

In Your name, amen

Week Eight

STUDENTS' INFLUENCES

CHALLENGE #8

Love in Action

*Little children, let us not love in word or
talk but in deed and in truth.*
— 1 JOHN 3:18 ESV

In my heart and my walk with Christ, I find it so important to love with my words. I was born a words of affirmation girl and feed off of the words of others, so my heart is to provide the same to those around me. If I tell you I love you, I do. If I tell you I appreciate you, I mean it. If I tell you how great of a job you are doing, it is sincere. I love others through my words.

But with that, I know when I am frustrated, upset, overwhelmed, etc. I show it with my attitude and my actions. I may not be purposefully rude or negative, but I shut down, keep to myself, or get short with others.

This verse speaks volumes to me because I know that so often, I can love in words and talk, and I can love in action and truth when I feel good and everything around me is well, but when things are not as I would like them, loving with my actions is hard. I know in difficult times, the sincerity of my words does not always show itself in my actions. And to be honest, ninety-nine percent of the time, I can notice when my actions aren't out of love, and I feel guilty about it, but I choose to stay in my funk.

As teachers, a lot is thrown on our plates and a lot can add up all at once. I know we all have days where coworkers make us upset or the lesson you planned for hours isn't going right or there's another meeting that you feel like you just don't have time for, and our emotions can get the best of our actions, and that is okay. We are human, but it doesn't mean we should stay that way.

The Lord calls us to love others in deed and truth.

So, what does that look like? In the workplace, it looks like praying for those around you, lifting one another up, bearing each other's burdens, having patience, understanding, and generosity. All of those things we hope our students learn and show are the things we should model as well.

Challenge #8- Love in Action

How can you show love in action this week? Words may be a small part of this, but dig deeper into your actions, the things you do for one another and with one another. Who can you pray for this week? Who can you lend a listening ear to? Where can you show generosity or kindness? When can you acknowledge the hard work of others? Where is an area in which you can show sincerity and truth to your school and your students?

Dear Lord,

I know that my words mean well, but my actions are not always done out of love or sincerity. I know there are areas in my life where I need to let go of some anger and resentment and begin showing an attitude and actions of love in my workplace. Words are so easy to throw around, but sincere actions show a true heart, Lord. A heart that seeks You first and loves above all else. Lord, show me areas where I can use my actions to show love to those around me this week. As I pray over some of the people closest to me in my school, make me aware of areas I need to be more sincere in my love. Show me ways I can use my actions and my words to be glorifying to You.

In Your name, amen

CAFETERIA WORKERS

For he satisfies the longing soul, and the hungry soul he fills with good things.
— PSALM 107:9 ESV

As I am writing this, the world is in a pandemic. A one in one hundred years thing. My county has just released for summer break, but teachers and students haven't been in the school buildings for months. We have taught online through digital learning platforms and made it work, but I am excited to have the summer off (as most teachers are!)

While teachers, students, support staff, etc. couldn't get into the school buildings, cafeteria workers across the county were still working to prepare lunches for students who needed them.

Every morning, they would come in and make sack lunches to be delivered across the county. I couldn't find exact numbers, but our county made and served about 25,000 lunches a day when students weren't even in the building!

During this pandemic, and all throughout the school year, cafeteria workers work so hard to make sure students and teachers have food that is safe and healthy. I can't imagine what we would do without them in our schools.

Today, pray for your cafeteria workers. Let them know you are praying for them and appreciate all of their hard work.

Dear Lord,

I lift up the cafeteria workers at my school and around our nation to You today, Lord. They work so hard to make sure students are fed a healthy meal for breakfast and lunch all year round. The women at my school always provide service with a smile and are willing to clean up after students whether they feel appreciated or not. I want to specifically thank them for feeding children who may not have food at home. Sometimes we know who these kids are, but other times we don't. No matter the circumstance, these children are fed at school with a smile.

I pray that You would provide purpose and joy in the lives of each of our cafeteria workers. Allow them to know they are making such a difference in the lives of students from so many different backgrounds and home lives. Allow them to feel appreciated by both students and teachers for their hard work each day, but most of all, help them know that they are loved by You and their work is good in Your eyes.

In Your name, amen

CUSTODIANS

But all things should be done decently and in order
— 1 CORINTHIANS 14:40 ESV

One of the most important pieces of advice from my husband when I first started teaching was "make friends with the custodians at your school." I wasn't sure why or what exactly he meant at the moment, but that was probably one of the best pieces of advice that year.

Kids are messy! Being an elementary school teacher, custodians are people I am so thankful for! I work in an old building, so there is a lot of cleaning that needs to be done just to keep the school looking and smelling normal.

I also can't even count the number of times custodians have had to clean the floors after projects and spills or brought the "big trash can" for all of the stuff (that's the nicest way I can put it) that comes in and out of my classroom.

I am sure middle and high school classrooms are just as messy, but maybe in a different way.

Custodians make sure our school is clean which keeps our students healthy and makes learning much easier. They disinfect, dust, vacuum, clean carpets, take out the trash etc. in not just our classrooms but around the whole school. They work so hard during the school year and over the summer (shout out to my favorite custodian for keeping my plant alive that I accidentally left all summer!).

Today, pray for your custodians and let them know you are praying for them and appreciate their hard work to keep our schools clean and our students and teachers healthy.

Dear Lord,

Today I want to thank You for the custodians at my school. I know they do so much for not only me, but everyone in the school building to keep our school in order and student's healthy. I never hear the custodians complain, no matter how much trash I have in my trash can or how many times I forget to put it outside the door before recess. They always work with a smile and are willing to do what they can to help.

I know there are days that they don't enjoy their job. It is demanding and to be honest, probably gross sometimes, but they work through it. Lord, I pray that You would help each custodian remember their job is so important and we couldn't survive as a school without them. Allow them to feel appreciated and important in our school. Lord, I pray You would help me do my part in helping them keep the school clean and organized and being a positive classroom for them to serve.

In Your name, amen

BUS DRIVERS

*The second is this: 'You shall love your neighbor as yourself.'
There is no other commandment greater than these.*
— MARK 12:31 ESV

There is no doubt that you have to love kids to be a teacher, and the same goes for bus drivers. For some children, a bus driver is the first smiling face they see in the morning and the last at the end of the day. Bus drivers wake up before the sun to check their busses each morning and pick up several routes of students. A quick break and they do the same thing in the evening, getting home well after we are done, or supposed to be done, for the day.

Each and every day, millions of kids are transported to and from school on school buses, and for those few moments each day, not only are bus drivers focused on student safety, they are also focused on building relationships with their students. They have a heart for their job, just like we do as teachers.

Parents and teachers put the lives of our students in the hands of bus drivers and trust them to keep each and every child safe.

Bus drivers hold such an important role and have such an impact on the lives of students every single day.

Today, pray for the bus drivers at your school and let them know that you are praying for them and appreciate all they do for students.

Dear Lord,

I come to You today to lift up the men and women who drive children on their school buses to and from school each and every day. I know that I don't know many of them by name, but they play such an important role in the lives of students at my school and schools around the country. I am thankful that these men and women put the lives of students as their top priority each morning and afternoon, making sure they arrive at school and home safely. I also am thankful that they work towards making relationships with students and putting smiles on their faces.

I pray that You would allow school bus drivers to know that their job is so important. Parents and teachers put their trust in the bus drivers each and every day. We appreciate their commitment towards working early in the morning and finishing up after we are done for the day. We are so thankful for all that they do. Keep them free from distraction and danger. Keep the joy of the job alive, allowing them to know the impact they make each and every day.

In Your name, amen

PARENTS

*Let your work be shown to your servants, and
your glorious power to their children.*
— PSALM 90:16 ESV

When thinking about the people involved in our schools, those who help teachers and students, teammates, administrators, custodians and cafeteria workers are at the top of that list, but parents also play a huge role in making our schools successful.

I never understood the necessity of a Parent Teacher Association (PTA) until I was about halfway through my first year teaching. All I knew is that I was highly encouraged to join PTA at the beginning of the year, and I bought a cute t-shirt to wear on spirit wear Fridays.

Later in the year I learned just how much they did for teachers from arranging fundraisers for new technology and playground equipment to planning lunches during conferences. Our PTA parents went above and beyond helping in the classrooms and advocating for our school, teachers and students.

I am so thankful for the parents in our community who want to be involved and support teaching. Their work has a huge impact on their students and shows the importance of education.

Dear Lord,

I want to pray for the parents of the students that I teach, specifically those who are involved at the school. I know that many parents work and don't have the option to help during school hours, but I am thankful for those who do have the ability to come and help where needed. These parents make our jobs so much easier. I am thankful for the money they help raise, for the lunches they prepare, and for their continued support in education.

I pray that You would let these parents know they are valued and appreciated for all of their hard work in supporting both students and teachers. I pray You would help keep their desire to serve alive and ignite a passion in other parents to participate where possible. I pray You would keep your hand on them, Lord, keep their families safe and healthy.

In Your name, amen

RESOURCE OFFICERS

*Blessed are the peacemakers, for they
shall be called sons of God.*
— MATTHEW 5:9 ESV

There are hundreds of groups of people in schools across the nation that support students every single day and each group deserves so much recognition, but I wanted to end this section by thanking and praying over the resource officers and police officers that work in and respond to situations at each of our schools.

Most of the time, we don't think about resource officers at our workplace. At my school we see them in the hallways and cafeteria talking to students and checking doors. To teachers and students, they are often just another friendly face around the building, and that's how we like it.

But they are working. They work in the background as an extra presence patrolling and surveilling our buildings. We know they are prepared for anything that comes towards them, and we acknowledge their work to keep our schools safe.

All the while, in the backs of teachers' minds, we pray we will never truly need a resource officer to step in and defend our school family. We pray there will never be a moment to see them in action. We pray that all their job consists of is ensuring our safety but never actually having to respond to a crisis.

Our hearts shutter at the thought of anything else, but the only thing we have control over is to thank them for all they do and pray that every time we see them, they are smiling and talking with our students.

Dear Lord,

My mind can not imagine anything besides the wonderful experiences that I have had with our school resource officers. I am beyond thankful for the role they play in our schools and keeping students safe. Lord, I pray that Your hand is always upon my school's SRO and every other officer across the nation. I pray that no matter what happens, You will ensure they are prepared and knowledgeable of how to handle any situation, especially those involving children. Keep our students safe. Keep our staff safe. Lord, we trust in You.

In Your name, amen

CHALLENGE #9

Your Light

You are the light of the world. A city set on a hill cannot be hidden. Nor do people light a lamp and put it under a basket, but on a stand, and it gives light to all in the house. In the same way, let your light shine before others, so that they may see your good works and give glory to your Father who is in heaven.
— MATTHEW 5:14-18 ESV

You are the light of the world. Your light can not be hidden. Let your light shine.

You have such an impact on your students. You are a light to them and to the rest of the world. God has placed you in the community where you are to share your light with your students and those around you. Use your influence. Embrace your influence. Cherish your influence.

Pray over your students. Love on them. Care for them.

BUT don't forget to take care of you!

Teaching can be all consuming. We are constantly thinking about our students and lesson plans and interventions and meetings and staff development. It is hard to turn our minds off of school even during the summer.

I am sure you are guilty, just like I am, of staying late when we know we need to get home or going home just to pick up our computers or ungraded papers and continue working. It's our instinct. We want to do everything we can for our students, so we pour our hearts and souls into what we do.

BUT You can't be a light if you aren't shining inside. You can't be a positive influence to others if you don't take care of yourself first. You can't pour from an empty cup.

Challenge #9- Your Light

This last section, though short, is so important. It is about looking inward, thinking about what you need, and taking care of you.

Take time to write down areas in which you know you could let go a little, areas where you might be overextending yourself, and areas in which you need to step back and take care of you first.

I know it's hard.

I am the first one to commit to more than I should, so I get it, but if that is you, ask God to give you the power to say "no" or "not right now" or "instead of… what about…"

One of my best teacher friends and mentor does a great job of saying "not right now. I'm taking care of me." I so admire that.

You are in control of your life and your decisions. You can't be a light to others if you aren't shining inside.

Dear Lord,

I know like many around me, I am glued to my job because I care and because I know the importance of what I do each day. My students and teaching is always on my mind and sometimes, it is hard to turn off, but I know that it is just as important to take care of me as it is to take care of my students.

Lord, help me to find places where I can take care of me and those I love most. Show me areas in which I may not be stewarding my gifts in the best way I can. Allow me to make decisions, even if they are tough, that will benefit me, my family, my students and my career. I want to be a light shining on a hill for You, but I know that comes with taking care of me and being close to You.

In Your name, amen

YOUR WALK

Trust in the Lord with all your heart, and do not lean on your own understanding. In all your ways acknowledge him, and he will make straight your paths.
— PROVERBS 3:5-6 ESV

Sometimes it's easy to pray for yourself. Sometimes it's hard and seems selfish. Even when we do pray for ourselves, we often pray about the things around us and within us rather than our walk and relationship with Christ.

It is just something that is supposed to be there. We are supposed to read our bibles, supposed to pray, supposed to have and share faith, but that doesn't mean we can't pray for those areas. We can absolutely pray for God to move in our lives. We can absolutely pray that He would guide us in building our relationship with Him.

I know sometimes I struggle with consistent quiet times with the Lord, but when I pray about that shortcoming and ask God to guide me, He always finds a way to point me towards my bible or wrestle with my heart until I stop and spend time with Him.

Trust in the Lord. Lean on His understanding.

Today, take time to pray for your walk and your relationship with Christ. Ask Him to strengthen it. Ask Him to nudge you in the areas you could improve upon and strengthen your relationship with Him.

Dear Lord,

Today I am thankful, Lord, that You are not only my Savior and my Heavenly Father, but You are also my friend. You are someone I can talk to and listen to. You speak to me, Lord, and I know Your words are filled with so much power. I pray that You would consistently remind me of the power of Your word and spending time with You.

My walk with You is so important, but can easily be pushed to the side, so I want to commit to making my time with You a priority.

Speak words of wisdom and encouragement to me, Lord. Show me areas I can come closer to You. Show me places in which I may put other things before You, so that I can rearrange my priorities. Open my heart to be willing to listen and crave the words You speak. Strengthen my walk with You. Strengthen my heart because everything else flows from it.

In Your name, amen

YOUR FAMILY

A devout man who feared God with all his household, gave alms generously to the people, and prayed continually to God.
— ACTS 10:2 ESV

You've prayed over your students and their families, but oh how important your families and children are as well.

Not only has God called you to be a teacher, but He has also called you to be a part of a family- a wife, husband, mom, dad, roommate, daughter, son, sister, or friend. Those jobs come first. Your family comes first.

You have family and friends that depend on you day in and day out.

And even if you don't have a husband and kids right now (I don't have kids of my own yet, except two pups), God has still called you to a family. He has given you people to go home to. He has given you people to love you and care for you as you do the same for them.

While this devotion is all about being a teacher and praying for your students, don't let teaching consume you. Your family is more important than your career.

Be with your family. Be a wife. Be a mom (or dog mom!). Be a roommate, a sister, a friend. Be there.

At the end of the year, your students will leave you, but your family will still be there needing you, and one of the best things you can do for them is be there.

Dear Lord,

There is not enough time in the day to pray for my family the way I know I should, but thank you. Thank You for giving me a family to go home to each night. Thank You for giving me parents and siblings and a husband and two wonderful puppies. I am so grateful that, although I have a calling to teach, it isn't my life. My career doesn't define who I am. At the end of the day, I want to put You and my family first.

Lord, I pray my family has understanding that being a teacher can be exhausting and overwhelming, but also one of the most rewarding professions. Allow me grace when I fall short of my responsibilities as a wife, and allow me to give grace because I know their jobs are just as challenging and demanding.

I pray for the health and wellbeing of my family. I pray for happiness and love, but most of all, I pray for a family rooted in You. Bless my family. Keep Your hands upon us.

In Your name, amen

YOUR REST

Jacob's well was there; so Jesus, wearied as he was from his journey, was sitting beside the well. It was about the sixth hour.
— JOHN 4:6 ESV

I am so passionate about teachers taking rest and taking care of their mental health, but I am also probably not the person to be talking about this. Like most teachers, I would rather go into work sick than find a sub, make sub plans, get everything set up, tell my team what to pull out for me, etc. It's a lot of work, and honestly, we are teachers because of our students, so if it is better for us to go in and be with our students, that is what we are going to do.

But whether I choose to take rest or not, God always finds a way to make me rest, typically in the most unusual ways, and no matter how annoyed I am, I am so thankful for the rest He provides. I need it. He knows I need it.

Whenever I am discouraged and think I just need to power through even when I am tired, I find comfort in knowing that even Jesus, the most powerful man in the world, the most perfect man to walk on this Earth, needed to rest, too.

John 4:6 says, "Jesus, wearied as he was from his journey, was sitting beside the well."

Jesus, weary from His journey, took a seat.

How many of you are weary from your journey? How many of you need to sit down and rest for a minute?

Teaching is your journey and teaching is exhausting. Don't forget to take time for yourself. It doesn't make you any less of a teacher. It doesn't make you any less of a teammate. Resting doesn't define who you are, but it will make you stronger and more prepared for the road ahead.

Dear Lord,

I am in awe of this verse and the reminder that even You get weary, even You sometimes need to rest. I thank You for the moments that You have given me rest, even when I wasn't sure I needed it or didn't want to take it. I am thankful for the things around me that provide comfort and security when this journey of life seems overwhelming. I am thankful for friends and family who put my physical health and mental health above my career and show me that I can do the same, Lord. I pray You would continue to provide me with opportunities to rest. Continue to nudge my heart when I am stubborn and want to push through. You know what is best, and You know that rest isn't a sign of weakness. Lord, You are not weak. But it is a part of life and it is okay to rest, just like You, Lord.

In Your name, amen

YOUR IMPACT

The heart of the wise makes his speech judicious and adds persuasiveness to his lips. Gracious words are like a honeycomb, sweetness to the soul and health to the body.
— PROVERBS 16:23-24 ESV

At the beginning of this prayer guide, I asked you about your calling or your purpose, why you started teaching and why you are in the school, grade level, position you are in. I also spoke about the influence of a teacher and asked you to think about the impact you are leaving on your students each day.

For almost a quarter of the year now, you have prayed for your students and for the people around you that impact students each and every day. I hope you continue to pray, but I also hope you remember the impact that you have on so many little lives in front of you.

Your students are watching you. Your students are listening to you. Your students are following you. What do you want them to learn? What do you want them to leave you knowing? What do you want them to grow up to be?

Beyond anything else, know that you matter to so many people. Your work is so important. You can make a difference in the life of a child, and even if you touch just one, how amazing that impact is!

Today, pray over your words, your actions, your thoughts. Pray over the lasting impact you have on your students. Pray God will use you in a mighty way.

Dear Lord,

I have said it before, and I will say it again. I am so honored and blessed that You chose me to be a teacher. It is not a job I take lightly. It is a job I pour my heart and soul into each and every day because I know I have an important responsibility to be a teacher, light, guide, and mentor to these students. I know that my words and actions matter, and I want to do everything I can to use them for good and for Your glory. I pray that You would use me, Lord. Remind me each day of the reason I became a teacher. Remind me how much You love the children You have placed in my classroom, and show me how to love them just as much. Let not my impact, but Your impact stick with these children as they grow.

In Your name, amen

YOUR LOVE

Beloved, let us love one another, for love is from God, and whoever loves has been born of God and knows God.
— 1 JOHN 4:7 ESV

The basis of this devotion and prayer guide is love, love for teaching, love for your students, love for your schools, love for your communities. Even during hard and trying seasons, love is all around us, and we are almost required to show love every day.

Love is what makes God who He is, and love is what drives the passion of what you and I do each and every day. We wouldn't want to teach if we didn't love teaching or love our students. We wouldn't be in our schools if we didn't love where we were at. We wouldn't have coworkers that turn into best friends without love surrounding us.

That doesn't mean everything is perfect and pleasant. It doesn't mean you aren't going to have bad days or defeating moments. It doesn't mean there are always going to be smiles and rainbows covering your classroom, but it does mean that God has provided us with a stronger force than anything we can imagine.

Love.

So, on this last day of prayer, hopefully hearts, students, schools and communities filled with love, take a second to recognize God's love toward you and your love for your students and your school. Be proud of who you are and what you do every single day. The love that you have poured out into your schools through prayer is remarkable. Don't take that lightly. Your love shines through YOU each and every day and what a beautiful thing it is.

Dear Lord,

I thank You for the heart of a teacher. It is a job like no other. A job that is demanding and overwhelming but also amazing and rewarding. We have the responsibility to raise up the next generation, in love. I pray throughout the rest of my years as a teacher, You would allow me to show more and more of Your love each day. Allow my students to see You in me. I hope they wonder what is different and find their way into Your open, loving arms.

In Your name, amen

MY PRAYER FOR YOU

To The Teacher Reading This,

The Lord bless you and keep you; the Lord make his face to shine upon you and be gracious to you; the Lord lift up his countenance upon you and give you peace.
— NUMBERS 6:24-26 ESV

You made it to the end! You committed to praying over your teacher heart, your students and your school and over these past few months, you have done just that!

Take a second and reflect on these last few months. Have you noticed a difference? Have you noticed God working in your life or the lives of your students or colleagues? Do you feel like your prayers made a difference? Do you see your students in a new light?

I know when I began praying over my students consistently, the biggest change was within my own heart. I was able to begin to see my students the way God sees them and begin to love them like God loves them. The good days seemed to be just a little bit better, and I felt more compassion and patience even on the hard days.

I pray this prayer guide has made a difference in your own life and your teaching practice. Don't let this journey stop here. I pray you would continue to pray over your students for the rest of this year and the years to come. They need your prayers. You are making a difference whether you see a difference or not.

I pray whether you've been teaching for two years or twenty years, that you would never lose your desire to teach the students God has given you. I pray you will feel a passion and purpose each day you wake up. I pray you will feel joy and peace stepping into your classroom.

I pray God's abundant love and grace would overflow you. I pray His strength would become your strength and His will, your will. I pray each day He would direct your steps and allow you a chance to share just a little bit more of His love.

I pray God would allow you to teach, serve, love, and mentor each one of the little lives that walks into your classroom, leaving a lasting impact on both those students and on your own heart. I pray He would change you for the better with each passing year.

I pray you would never lose the love of impacting lives each and every single day. That you will know the importance of your job and the work you do each day.

I pray God would grant you rest and peace when you need it most. Be willing to take a break and step back from the chaos. Allow yourself grace when things seem overwhelming or uncertain.

God's got you. God's called you to this place. He won't leave you.

Never forget how amazing the gift to teach is and how amazing it is that God chose you to raise up the next generation.

I can't wait to hear what God has prepared for you and your students.

Love, Hannah England

READER'S DISCUSSION GUIDE

Week One

1. What is your reason or purpose for teaching? Why are you a teacher? Why are you reading this book? Why do you want to pray over your students and school?
2. How did you know God was calling you to be a teacher? How did you end up in the district, school, grade level, or subject you are teaching? Can you see God's hand in bringing you to this place?
3. What vision do you hope God gives you over these next few weeks?

Week Two

1. What are your hopes and goals for praying over your students? What are the short-term goals you hope to see over these next few weeks? What are the long-term goals you hope for their futures?
2. What obstacles do you see getting in your way of prayer and time with God? What are practical solutions to help you meet your goals?
3. How can you best pray for the minds of your students? How can you model and encourage patience, positivity, perseverance, confidence and humility in your classroom?

Week Three

1. What is your class like? How would you define your group of students this year? Why do you use those words in describing them?
2. Knowing your class and your students, what do you think God might be trying to teach you with this group of students?

133

3. How can you best pray for the hearts of your students? How can you model and encourage respect, kindness, generosity, gratitude, and leadership in your classroom?

Week Four

1. How do you keep track of what you know about your students and the new information you learn? Are you continuing to learn about your students each day?
2. Are there any students you know you need to learn more about? How can you dig deeper in finding out who they are, what they are interested in, and who they want to grow up to be?
3. How can you best pray for the souls of your students? How can you model and encourage self control, responsibility, wisdom, forgiveness, and honesty in your classroom?

Week Five

1. What are some immediate areas of need you can identify within your classroom and community- food, water, shelter, love? What can you do to support those areas of need?
2. There may be areas of need that you are not aware of. How can you open your eyes and heart to hear from God?
3. How can you best pray over the basic needs of your students? Can you ask God above and beyond those basic needs? What are your biggest hopes for your students?

Week Six

1. How do you pray for your students after they leave your classroom? Do you continue to pray for them as they grow older, change schools, and follow their own paths?
2. Do you bottle up prayers for the future of the students you are currently teaching? What do you hope their lives look like? What areas would you love to see God move?

3. In what areas do your students need to grow right now and in the future? Emotionally? Physically? Socially? Academically? What can you do to encourage and promote positive growth within each of your students?

Week Seven

1. In your school family, who do you do a really great job of showing your appreciation for? Who do you appreciate, but don't let them know? Is there anyone that it is hard to appreciate? What practical steps can you take towards showing your appreciation to all three of these groups?
2. Because you spend the most time with your teammates, how can you show them you care? What are their love languages? Do they like small gifts or words of affirmation? What is one thing you can do this week for your teammates to let them know you love them and appreciate all they do?
3. How can you specifically pray for those you may not know as well in your building? Who do you feel God calling you to reach out to and get to know? Is there a way you could be more accountable for getting to know your school? Could you bring breakfast or treats one day? Could you organize an outing or after school activity?

Week Eight

1. What does "love in action" look like to you? How can you show others you love and appreciate them with both your words and your actions?
2. Is there an area where you fall short in showing love? Is there some part of you that has a difficult time showing others love when you don't feel loved yourself? How can you change your attitude and perspective to one that shows and gives love no matter the circumstance?

3. Who are the other groups of people in your school building that you want to recognize and appreciate? How can you show them your appreciation?

Week Nine

1. How are you taking care of yourself? How are you nurturing and protecting your own teacher heart amongst all the craziness surrounding you? What are the little things you enjoy doing that fill your own heart and make your light shine brighter?

2. How is your walk with God? Is it a priority? Are you giving God the first and best of everything you have and then giving to others? Where does your family fall on your priority list? Do you show you value both of these above your career by your actions?

3. Are there any areas that you can let go of to protect your mental and physical health? Is there anything you have room for in your life that you want to give a try? How can you make sure your actions and activities are aligned with your priorities?

ESV BIBLE VERSE INDEX

The Old Testament

Genesis 1:29	69
Exodus 18:21	101
Numbers 6:24-26	131
Deuteronomy 32:2	5
Job 8:7	79
Psalm 20:4	17
Psalm 90:16	113
Psalm 107:9	107
Psalm 127:3-4	65
Proverbs 1:5	11
Proverbs 3:5-6	121
Proverbs 9:10	53
Proverbs 16:9	85
Proverbs 16:23-24	127
Proverbs 17:17	67
Proverbs 17:22	21
Proverbs 18:15	73
Proverbs 19:1	57
Proverbs 27:17	93
Proverbs 31:26	35
Ecclesiastes 3:12	83
Ecclesiastes 4:9-12	91
Jeremiah 29:11	77
Jeremiah 32:17	61

The New Testament

Matthew 5:9	115
Matthew 5:14-18	119
Matthew 7:12	33
Matthew 20:26	97
Mark 12:31	111
Luke 6:40	7
John 4:6	125
John 8:32	57
John 13:4-5	41
Acts 10:2	123
Acts 20:35	37
Romans 12:5	45
Romans 12:12	19
Romans 14:12	51
1 Corinthians 6:19	81
1 Corinthians 14:40	109
1 Corinthians 15:58	9
2 Corinthians 5:1	71
Galatians 6:9	19 & 23
Ephesians 2:10	31
Ephesians 4:32	55
Philippians 4:13	25
Colossians 3:23-24	95
1 Thessalonians 5:11	99
1 Thessalonians 5:16-18	39
Titus 2:7-8	xv
Hebrews 11:1	87
James 5:13	13
1 John 3:18	105
1 John 4:7	129
1 Peter 4:10	3
1 Peter 5:6	27
2 Timothy 1:7	49

ABOUT THE AUTHOR

Hannah Brooke England, wife and dog mama of two, is a third grade teacher passionate about the social emotional well-being of both teachers and students. She holds a bachelor's degree in K–5 general and special education from the University of North Georgia, a master's degree in gifted education from the University of Georgia, and has earned her endorsements in reading, gifted, and ESOL. Hannah shares her heart for loving, learning, and leading each day.